PERMANENT INTERNATIONAL COMMITTEE OF
LINGUISTS

A Bibliography of South African Languages, 2008-2017

Published by the Permanent International Committee of
Linguists under the auspices of the International Council for
Philosophy and Humanistic Studies

Edited by

Anne Aarssen, René Genis & Eline van der Veken

with an introduction by

Menán du Plessis

BRILL

LEIDEN | BOSTON

2018

The production of this book has been generously sponsored by the Stichting Bibliographie Linguistique, Leiden.

Cover illustration: the name of the Constitutional Court building (Johannesburg) written in eleven official languages of South Africa.

Library of Congress Control Number: 2018947044

Typeface for the Latin, Greek, and Cyrillic scripts: "Brill". See and download: brill.com/brill-typeface.

ISBN 978-90-04-37660-1 (paperback)
ISBN 978-90-04-37662-5 (e-book)

CONTENTS*

General works

General linguistics and related disciplines

---

* Please note that this collection is a thematic extract from the *Linguistic Bibliography* annual volumes and that certain sections falling outside of its scope were omitted.

CONTENTS

Indo-European languages

Languages of Mainland Southeast Asia

Languages of Sub-Saharan Africa

Pidgins and Creoles

CONTENTS

Sign languages

INTRODUCTION

Menán du Plessis

Opening remarks[1]

The publication of the specially curated *Bibliography of South African Languages* comes at a moment well-timed for reflection, not only on the past ten years of work on South African languages, but more broadly on developments in South African linguistics since the ending of apartheid, now nearly three decades ago. As Marc Greenberg remarks in his introduction to Brill's *Bibliography of Slavic Linguistics*,[2] 'capturing even a decadal slice in the manifold directions in which the field is moving is a fool's errand'. Certainly this is true of South African linguistics as well, and only the broadest contemporary themes can be highlighted here. These notes begin with a description of the linguistic landscape of the southern African region as a whole, and includes discussion of officially recognised languages; the status of post-colonial languages; and other languages spoken in the various countries of the region. The second section offers a brief summary of the history of linguistic studies specifically in South Africa, so as to explain the background against which more recent work may be assessed. The third section touches on the overall pattern of post-apartheid publications; while the fourth focuses more particularly on the past ten years up to the present, identifying some of the major trending topics of the moment.

The linguistic landscape of the southern African region

For purposes of this overview, southern Africa is taken to mean more or less the region southward of the latitudinal line that lies 15 degrees south of the equator.

---

1 Thanks to Bonny Sands for useful comments and additional suggestions for references.

2 http://bibliographies.brillonline.com/browse/bibliography-of-slavic-linguistics.

INTRODUCTION

This immense area includes southern areas of **Angola** and **Mozambique**, and the whole of **Namibia, Botswana, Zimbabwe, South Africa, Swaziland** and **Lesotho.** Occasional reference will be made to the southernmost parts of **Zambia** and **Malawi,** and briefly also to **Madagascar** and **Mauritius.**

Three key points to bear in mind throughout the discussion that follows are:

- The transfrontier distributions of most of the region's languages
- The dialectal complexity of individual languages
- The typical multilingualism of individual speakers, particularly in urban centres

The list in the left-hand column in Figure 1 gives some indication of the transfrontier distributions of selected major languages of African origin that are spoken in southern Africa, while the map alongside shows the location of the various countries mentioned in the list or in the course of this introduction. The map also indicates some of the areas used in Guthrie's system of zonal distributions for the NTU (or Bantu)[3] languages (Maho 2009).

(i) Officially recognised (and for the most part major) languages of the region

The terms 'official' and 'national' are sometimes used in connection with languages as though they are interchangeable. In the case of the southern African countries that give official (constitutional) recognition to a range of languages, the term 'national' may be invoked in the sense only that a particular language is spoken by a significant section of the nation's citizens – not necessarily by everyone, or as a language of national unity. This recognition may embody a formal obligation on the part of the state to provide for and support the use of the acknowledged languages (at least on a regional basis) in contexts such as basic education and the delivery of social services. At the

---

3 It was W. H. G. Bleek (for example 1862: 3) who introduced the use of 'Bantu' as the label for a vast sub-group of related African languages. The term much later acquired derogatory connotations, following its use by white South Africans as a misplaced way of referring to black people. Various alternatives have been proposed (such as Kintu, Sintu or Benue-Congo B), but few have gained traction. By way of compromise, the bare root only is used here, and is also (non-conventionally) written in capital letters, to emphasise its status as an abstract label.

Selected southern African languages of African origin, with names of the countries where they are predominantly spoken
NTU languages*
Wambo [R20]; Herero [R30] (*Angola, Namibia*)
Shona [S10] (*Zimbabwe*)
Tsonga [S50] (*Mozambique, South Africa*)
Venda [S20] (*South Africa*)
Sotho-Tswana [S30] (Tswana, Kgalagadi, N Sotho, S Sotho) (*Botswana, Lesotho, South Africa*)
Nguni [S40] (Ndebele, Zulu, Xhosa, Swati) (*South Africa, Swaziland, Zimbabwe*)
*Guthrie zones as per Maho (2009)
KHOE, JU, TUU languages
KHOE (Dama, Nama, Giri, Kora; Naro, Khwe, ǁGana, Shua, Tshwa) (*Angola, Namibia, Botswana, South Africa, Zimbabwe*)
JU (Juǀ'hoan, !Xun) (*Angola, Namibia, Botswana*)
TUU (ǀXam, Nǀuu, !Xoon) (*Botswana, South Africa*)

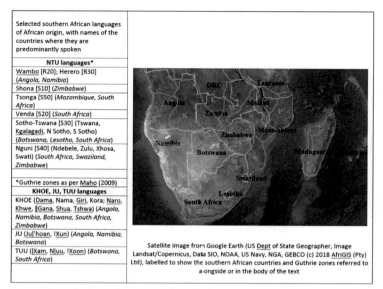

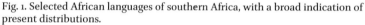

Satellite image from Google Earth (US Dept of State Geographer, Image Landsat/Copernicus, Data SIO, NOAA, US Navy, NGA, GEBCO (c) 2018 AfriGIS (Pty) Ltd), labelled to show the southern African countries and Guthrie zones referred to alongside or in the body of the text

Fig. 1. Selected African languages of southern Africa, with a broad indication of present distributions.

same time, for most countries of the region, the de facto official language – and sometimes even the formally declared one – is a language of colonial origin.

While they are by no means as rich in linguistic diversity as many other African countries, South Africa and Zimbabwe respectively give official recognition to twelve and sixteen national languages, where the vast majority belong to sub-groups of the immense NTU family (which is itself of course only a sub-division of just one branch of Niger-Congo). The official languages of **South Africa**,[4] apart from the two post-colonial and locally naturalised languages, English and Afrikaans, are: Tsonga (Shangaan) [S53], Venda [S21], Tswana [S31], Northern Sotho [S32], Sotho [S33], Ndebele [S47], Zulu [S42], Xhosa [S41], and Swati [S43]. In March of this year, South Africa also gave official recognition to South African Sign language (*SA Government News Agency*, 2018).[5]

---

4   The Constitution of South Africa is available online from: https://www.gov .za/documents/constitution/constitution-republic-south-africa-1996-1.

5   Online press release (https://www.sanews.gov.za/south-africa/sign-language -recognised-home-language), March 4 2018.

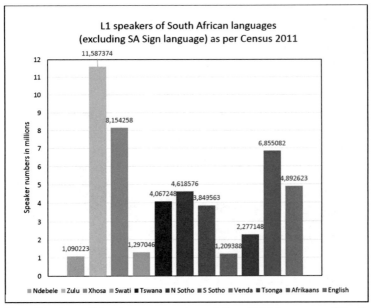

Fig. 2. Numbers of first language speakers of the official languages of South Africa, excluding SA Sign language. The total population of South Africa recorded in 2011 was 51,770,560.

The chart in Figure 2, based on the most recent census figures (*SA Census 2011, Census in Brief*: 23),[6] gives an indication of the numbers of first language speakers for each of the official languages of South Africa, except for SA Sign language.[7] As mentioned at the outset, though, most inhabitants of southern African countries – particularly those who live in urban centres – are multilingual, and

6   Latest census reports for South Africa are available online from: http://www .statssa.gov.za

7   Users of SA Sign language were enumerated in the 2011 census at 234,655, which may be an under-reporting, however, given controversies around the use of signing. The number of deaf people in the country is about 600,000 (pers. comm. from Jabaar Mohamed, Provincial Director, DeafSA Western Cape, April 5 2018).

typically speak one or more of the other languages as additional languages, with a variable degree of personal proficiency (Lanham 1978: 17).

Clause 6 of the constitution of **Zimbabwe**,[8] declares that the officially recognised languages of that country include the following, where the symbols in square brackets allude to Guthrie's distributional zones (as updated Maho 2009):[9] Shona [S11–S14], Ndau [S15], Kalanga [S16A], Nambya [S16B], Tonga [M64], Chewa (Cewa) [N30], Chibarwe [N45], Shangani [S53], Venda [S20], Tswana [S31], Sotho [S33], Ndebele (of Zimbabwe) [S44], and Xhosa [S41]. Further languages given official recognition in Zimbabwe are English, 'Koisan' [so-spelled], and Zimbabwean Sign language.

Article 3 of the constitution of **Namibia**[10] explicitly declares that English is the official language of the country, even though the most recent census figures indicate that it is spoken as a first language in only 3.4 percent of households. The Namibian document goes on to state that nothing contained in the constitution 'shall prohibit the use of any other language as a medium of instruction'. This means in effect that entry-level schooling may be (and indeed is) offered in Namibian Khoekhoe in the southern part of the country, with English being introduced to young learners a few grades later. In the most recent census (*Namibia Census 2011, Main Report*: 172),[11] the languages enumerated – in addition to English, Afrikaans, German, 'other European', and 'other African' – included: Wambo [R21, R22], Herero [R31], Kavango (various NTU languages), Caprivi (various NTU languages), San (probably varieties of JU and TUU, plus some western Kalahari KHOE),[12] Namibian Khoekhoe (KHOE) and Tswana [S31]. The labels 'Kavango' and 'Caprivi' are rather non-specific, but since they are contrasted with the equally vague term 'San', it is probable that they refer to various NTU languages spoken in the eastward-pointing arm of northern Namibian territory known as the Caprivi Strip. Languages spoken in

---

8   The Constitution of Zimbabwe is available online from: http://www.zim .gov.zw/constitution

9   The names of individual languages are given in their commonly accepted Anglicised forms.

10   The Constitution of Namibia is available online from: https://laws .parliament.na/namibian-constitution/

11   Latest census reports for Namibia are available online from: https://nsa .org.na/

12   The different families subsumed under the label 'Khoisan' are discussed in sub-section (iii).

the Strip – sections of which are contiguous with Angola, Zambia, Zimbabwe and Botswana – include: Yeyi [R41A], the Botatwe languages [M60] formerly Subiya-Totela [K40]: Fwe [K402], Totela [K41] and Subiya [K40]; (possibly) some varieties of Luyana [K31]; Kavango languages such as Kwangali [K33] and Gciriku (or Manyo) [K331/2]; and Mbukushu [K43].

While the constitution of **Botswana**[13] does not include a language clause, the report for the 2011 census (*Statistics Botswana 2014*: 261)[14] shows that in addition to English and Afrikaans, the languages enumerated included among others: Tswana [S31], Kgalagadi [S311], Herero [R31], Yeyi (of Ngamiland) [R41B], Subiya [K40], Mbukushu [K43], Zezuru [S12], Kalanga (of Botswana) [S16] and Ndebele [S408].

(ii)   A note on the status of post-colonial languages

As remarked above, for most countries of the region, the effective official language of government (and sometimes even the formally declared one) is a language of colonial origin. Throughout the region, access to tertiary education is entirely dependent on competence in one of the former colonial languages, such as English, Portuguese or French.

While English is perhaps most often still acquired only as a second language, other former colonial languages, such as Dutch and French, have long been established as naturalised local languages, with their daughters – in such forms, for example, as Afrikaans and Morisien (the French of **Mauritius**) – widely spoken as first languages by a sizeable proportion of the population in their respective countries. It is probable that some varieties of the Portuguese spoken in **Angola** and **Mozambique**, as well as the French spoken in countries such as **Madagascar**, the **Democratic Republic of the Congo** (DRC) and the **Central African Republic** (CAR) are similarly naturalised, although detailed information is not readily available.

At the same time there are ongoing shifts, as in the case of South African English, which seems, at least on anecdotal evidence, to be favoured increasingly as a first language by families whose most recent ancestors spoke Afrikaans or

---

13   The Constitution of Botswana is available online from: http://www.gov .bw/en/Tools--Services/Constitution-and-Laws-of-Botswana/.

14   Latest census reports for Botswana are available online from: http:// botswana.opendataforafrica.org/thpzhqb/botswana-census-data.

one of the other South African languages. The great majority of South Africans who can speak English still have it, however, only as a second or third language.[15]

(iii)   Other languages (for the most part minor ones) spoken in the region

Apart from the languages mentioned above, a number of other languages are spoken in southern African countries today, where most (but not all) are languages of African origin, with present-day distributions that sometimes reflect a long-established status quo of great historical complexity, and at other times reflect migrations of either a recent or not too distant past. Many (but certainly not all) of these are minority languages, in the twin sense of having not only relatively low speaker numbers, but also a generally marginal status in the countries where they are spoken.

The most remarkable of these other languages is perhaps Malagasy, the Austronesian language that functions as one of the official languages of **Madagascar**, along with French. This is one example of a language that is by no means minor, given that varieties of it are spoken as a first language by almost all 18 million Madagascans (*SIL Ethnologue*).[16] Questions such as when, how and why early maritime traders from South-east Asia first settled the island remain the subject of ongoing archaeological, historical and linguistic investigation.

Another intriguing case involves the great diaspora from South Africa that occurred in the second and third decades of the 19th century. The reasons for this voluntary exodus are complex, although aggressive colonial incursion is acknowledged to have been a primary impetus. The outcomes of these migrations include the presence today of Ndebele speakers in the Matabeleland region of southern **Zimbabwe**. While it is closely related to varieties of South African Ndebele, the Zimbabwean variety has some features of its own. In **Malawi**, the minor language known as Ngoni [N12] is thought to have had a similar origin in the migration of Nguni-speaking people from South Africa. On the other hand, a further group of people known as the Kololo, who spoke a Sotho-like language, migrated to the Barotseland region of the country known

---

15   Although the term 'Black South African English' is occasionally used to describe the English used as a second language by black South Africans, it does not connote any homogeneous 'variety'. There does not seem to be any single variety of English spoken uniquely by black South Africans who use it as a first language.

16   All references to the *SIL Ethnologue* are to the online edition (https://www.ethnologue.com), at April 6 2018.

today as **Zambia**, where they conquered local inhabitants who were known as the Lozi (Rozwi or Rotse). The language referred to today as Lozi [K20] reflects a strong Sotho influence. It is now found as a minor language also in Zimbabwe and Botswana (*SIL Ethnologue*). The Luyana dialects [K31] of south-western Zambia may have been part of an original (non-Sotho) Lozi group, but the picture is far from clear.

In more recent times, the situation has begun to reverse, and more and more people from other African countries now migrate to **South Africa**, whether to study, seek work, operate as traders, or buy goods for retailing back at home. Figures in general are unreliable, since immigrants may be uncertain of their legal status and hence reluctant to declare themselves, while many may simply come and go on a regular basis. It is sometimes suggested, however, that the number of expatriate Zimbabweans currently living in South Africa may be over a million. While most are probably speakers of a Ndebele variety, the *SIL Ethnologue* gives a figure of 18,000 for immigrant speakers of Shona in South Africa. Raj Mesthrie (2002:12) mentions the existence in Durban of somewhat older enclaves of people who trace their presence in South Africa back to the 1870s, and who still speak some Makhuwa (Makua) [P30] and Yao [P20]. These are both languages primarily of Mozambique, although they also have cross-border distributions into neighbouring countries.

The diverse Khoisan languages of southern Africa constitute an important section of the region's minority African languages. As most readers are probably aware, the terms 'Khoi' (also 'Khoikhoi' or 'Khoekhoen') and 'San' refer to traditional ethnological rather than any linguistic distinctions. The Khoi, who typically spoke varieties of Khoekhoe KHOE,[17] were herders; while the San, who spoke a wide range of languages, including some that in fact belong to the KHOE family,[18] were mostly restricted to an economic lifestyle

---

17 The use of capital letters for the names of these different families is not a standard convention, but is adopted here in the interest of clarity. In writing the names of individual languages, it is occasionally necessary to use the current IPA symbol for a click. Although it is generally undesirable to introduce 'exotic' symbols in this way, the languages in question never acquired commonly accepted English versions of their names.

18 Languages belonging to the Kalahari branch of the KHOE family were referred to by Dorothea Bleek (1927) as 'Central Bushman'. Westphal (1963) re-named them the Tshu-Khwe languages, after the terms commonly used for 'person' in different sub-groups. Vossen (1997) referred

based on hunting and gathering.[19] There are three long-recognised divisions of the Khoisan languages of southern Africa, where these are commonly referred to – in the terms devised by Ernst Westphal (1963) – as KHOE, JU and !Ui-Taa. For the latter, the alternative name TUU has more recently been suggested by Tom Güldemann (2004a). A few re-groupings have been proposed by one or two linguists in recent years, but these remain controversial.[20] The question of a common ancestry for the three families also continues to be debated, and the blanket term 'Khoisan' is currently used only as a general term of convenience.

Representatives of the different families, KHOE, JU and TUU, are today found mainly in **Namibia** and **Botswana**, but to a limited extent also in southern **Angola**, south-western **Zimbabwe**, and **South Africa**. Two unrelated click languages, Hadza and Sandawe, are spoken further afield, in **Tanzania**. (The last two appear to be isolates, however, and no strong evidence has been found to suggest a relation between either of them and any of the Khoisan languages of southern Africa.)

The Khoisan languages spoken in southern **Angola** are varieties of !Xun (JU), and varieties of Khwe (western Kalahari KHOE). In the case of these Angolan languages, it is difficult to obtain a clear sense of speaker numbers. In **Namibia**, the most recent census figures (*Namibia Census 2011 Main Report*: 172) reveal that varieties of Namibian Khoekhoe are spoken in 11 percent of households, out of a total population of just over two million. The number of households where 'San' was spoken amounted to 0.8 percent – where the generic term 'San' probably encompasses languages belonging to the KHOE family, such as Khwe and Naro (both Kalahari branch), as well as varieties from the TUU and JU families.

---

to them as 'non-Khoekhoe Khoe', but this was later replaced by 'Kalahari Khoe' (Güldemann and Vossen 2000).

19   Cruder distinctions between Khoi and San based on colonial perceptions of supposed biological differences are sometimes still alluded to by foreign scholars, but approaches of this kind – even when re-cast as 'genetic studies' – are offensive to South Africans, who view them as the uncritical perpetuation of an older ideology.

20   A link between the JU group and ǂʼAmkoe (also known as Eastern ǂHoan) has been proposed by Heine and Honken (2010), who offer the name KX'A for the unified group. A connection between the KHOE family and the Angolan isolate Kwadi has been proposed by Güldemann (2004b).

INTRODUCTION

The country with the greatest diversity of Khoisan languages (if not numbers of speakers) is certainly **Botswana**. Despite this, the report for the most recent census in Botswana (*Statistics Botswana 2014*: 261) indicates that in addition to the various other languages enumerated, there was just a single category provided for 'Sesarwa'. As Andy Chebanne (2008) pointed out concerning the previous census of 2001, the term 'Sesarwa' is merely a catch-all label for numerous different languages spoken by people from those communities formerly referred to collectively (and disparagingly) as 'Masarwa'. These languages include several that belong to the KHOE family, such as varieties of Khwe, Naro, ǁGana-ǀGui, Shua and Tshwa (all divisions of Kalahari KHOE), as well as Juǀʼhoan (JU) and !Xoon (Taa TUU). In the latest census, the total number of speakers of 'Sesarwa' amounted to just over 31,700, or 1.6 percent of the total Botswana population, which, much like that of Namibia, is a little over two million people.

Khoisan languages in **South Africa** are formally acknowledged in the country's new constitution, where they are mentioned in a sub-clause as minority languages entitled to official support (although the principle is rather undermined by the muddled reference to 'the Khoi, Nama and San languages'). In reality, the only viable Khoisan language still found in South Africa today is the Nama variety (Khoekhoe KHOE) of the far Northern Cape. The exact number of speakers is not known, but is unlikely to be more than 5,000, and is probably far less. It is spoken in addition to Afrikaans and with varying degrees of fluency by only one in four or five elderly people, mainly in Riemvasmaak and the Richtersveld (Witzlack-Makarevich 2006: 12). In recent years, in an attempt to revitalise it, the language has been introduced as a subject at selected junior schools in the area. There were also still (as of April 2018) one or two elderly rememberers of another Khoekhoe variety, namely Kora (Korana or !Ora); as well as three elderly speakers of Nǀuu (!Ui TUU).

With the ending in 1990 of the Border War, members of various San communities originally from southern Angola had to be relocated to South Africa. This was necessary because some of them had served with the SA military (that is, on the side of the apartheid regime) in the Kavango and Caprivi areas. These refugees include speakers of Khwe dialects (Kalahari KHOE) as well as !Xun dialects (JU) – none of which are indigenous to South Africa.

The constitution of **Zimbabwe** makes a concession to a vaguely denoted 'Koisan language', although the only relevant language still spoken in that country is a variety known as Tcuaʼo (Tjwao, Tshwao or Tcoao), which belongs to the KHOE family (eastern Kalahari), and had only eight remaining speakers as of March 2018.

A small fraction of the additional minor languages found in southern African countries today are of foreign but non-colonial origin, where these are generally spoken only by recent immigrants.[21] The *SIL Ethnologue* entry for South Africa, for example, includes the following in its list of immigrant languages, with speaker numbers in parentheses: Anglo-Romani (7,900), Arabic (5,000), Dutch (30,000), Mandarin Chinese (10,000), German (45,000) and Yue Chinese (15,000).

Historical background to linguistic studies in South Africa, 1960 to 1990

From this point onward, the focus of this overview will be limited largely to **South Africa**. There are several comprehensive older surveys (Doke 1945; Doke 1961a; Doke 1961b; Cole 1960; Cole 1971) that more than adequately recount the early history of language studies and linguistics in South Africa, and there is no need to recapitulate them here. The following notes pick up the story from the early 1960s, from the period just over a century after the arrival of Wilhelm Bleek in South Africa in the middle of the 19th century and the commencement of his pioneering work on both NTU and Khoisan languages.

One of the most striking aspects of the work of the earlier South African linguists of the 20th century, exemplified in the work of Clement Doke, is the wide-ranging focus of their work, not merely on languages of their own country, but on languages of the southern African region as a whole. On the whole, this breadth of vision seems to have became steadily narrowed from the 1960s up until the end of the 1980s – in step with the hardening of apartheid, and the increasing ostracism of South Africa by the international community. Nonetheless, there were certainly some notable exceptions to this general trend.

Although the policy of apartheid was officially inaugurated in 1948, the roll-out of the various laws intended to implement it took some time. Beginning in the 1960s, these laws began to bite ever more viciously into society, so that the minority white government found itself increasingly confronted with popular

---

21   The indentured labourers who were shipped by the British to Natal from India between 1860 and 1911 brought with them various Indic and Dravidian languages, such as Hindi, Urdu, Gujarati and Konkani; and Tamil and Telugu respectively (Mesthrie 2002: 12). These languages are on the wane, if they are still spoken at all. Descendants of these communities speak what is sometimes referred to as 'Indian South African English'.

resistance and, from 1966 onwards, outright military conflict beyond its borders, with the allied liberation movements of South Africa, Namibia and Angola. It is remarkable that Ernst Westphal was able to carry on conducting fieldwork as freely as he did during the 1960s, travelling throughout countries in the southern African region, and documenting a wide range of languages, both NTU and Khoisan.[22]

Despite the manifest inequities entrenched by apartheid, it was part of the inexorable logic of 'separate but equal development' that African languages should be given full support as languages of education, at least in the early years, during which stage mother-tongue education was believed to be in the best interest of the child.[23] This meant that there should be at very least pedagogic and reference grammars as well as dictionaries available for all of the major African languages spoken in the country; and it may be for this reason that one contemporary survey (Lanham 1978: 16) reported so positively on the development of these languages. R. A. Paroz published one of several revisions and enlargements of the older *Southern Sotho–English Dictionary* of Adolphe Mabille and H. Dieterlin (1961); while a revised and transliterated edition of the *Xhosa–English Dictionary* of J. McLaren (1963) was prepared by W. G. Bennie and J. J. R. Jolobe. Westphal's graduate student Jan Snyman (1970) delivered the first full-length grammatical description of Jul'hoan (JU), and went on to publish a dictionary (Jul'hoan–Afrikaans) in about 1975. Dirk Ziervogel and Enos Mabuza (1976) gave us a reference grammar for Swati; and J. A. Louw and J. B. Jubase (1978) delivered one for Xhosa, written in Afrikaans. Meanwhile, Gabriel Nienaber and P. E. Raper (1977, 1980), with admirable disregard for the prejudices of the time, laboured to produce a three-volume work on the Khoekhoe origins of more than 4,000 place-names of South Africa and Namibia.

It was also during the apartheid period that some of the first professional associations representing branches of linguistics in South Africa were

---

22 The bulk of Westphal's field material was never published, but his manuscript notes and recordings have been digitised and are now available online (http://www.digitalcollections.lib.uct.ac.za).

23 The policy was then (as it is today) that children should be introduced to either English or Afrikaans from about the third or fourth grade, and that their other subjects should be taught increasingly from then onward in one of those languages. When the apartheid government did away with the choice and made the medium of instruction obligatorily Afrikaans, the resulting fury led to the famous Soweto uprising of 1976.

established. These included, in 1966, SAALT, the South African Association for Language Teaching (publishing the *Journal for Language Teaching*); in 1979, ALASA, the African Language Association of Southern Africa (publishing the *South African Journal of African Languages*); and in 1980, SAALA, the Southern African Applied Linguistics Association, and LSSA, the Linguistics Society of South Africa (publishing *Southern African Linguistics and Applied Language Studies*).[24]

The 1980s were a paradoxical time for South African linguistics. On one hand, some breakthrough scholarly work appeared. For example, D. K. Rycroft (1981) published a dictionary for Swati; Alan Barnard (1985) published his wordlist for Naro (Kalahari KHOE); and Anthony Traill (1985) published his landmark study of the phonetics and phonology of !Xoon (Taa TUU family). E. J. M. Baumbach (1987) published his *Analytical Tsonga Grammar;* and Nienaber (1989) continued to produce encyclopaedic work on aspects of the old Cape Khoekhoe dialects.

On the other hand, it was only now, at the very late date of 1983, that one of the country's leading universities finally established a department of linguistics. Throughout the country, linguists at the better universities (which were typically those reserved for 'white people') tended to focus almost exclusively on varieties of English or Afrikaans. This somewhat self-absorbed approach was perhaps partly in response to the growing exclusion of South Africa at this time from the international academic community. What is more, and reflecting a similar parochialism, almost every grandly styled 'department of African languages' of this period typically offered only one or two languages! (As most linguists are aware, Africa is home to perhaps as many as 2000 languages.)

And it was all at this very same time that mass resistance to apartheid was swelling within the country into a hugely dynamic movement. Rallies with thousands upon thousands of participants became regular events, and there can hardly have been a university that did not experience tear gas drifting across its lawns, or did not have to cope with violent clashes between its own students and invading police in full riot gear. Towards the close of the decade, it was clear that the end of apartheid was in sight; and suddenly it seemed possible to start imagining a transformed academia in South Africa – one that would be less turned in on itself, and more reflective of a greater, African identity.

---

24   First published in 1980 – but as volume 18, since it represented the amalgamation of two older journals, *South African Journal of Linguistics* (LSSA) and *Southern African Journal of Applied Language Studies* (SAALA).

INTRODUCTION

South African linguistics in the post-apartheid era

There have undoubtedly been some high points in the study of southern African languages over the past two or three decades. The level of academic productivity is even high enough that it becomes invidious to single out any particular authors while overlooking others! It is unlikely, though, that anyone will begrudge the special mention of a few selected publications. Work on South African languages that particularly springs to mind include the reference grammar for Venda (Poulos 1990); the first combined version of the older English–Zulu and Zulu–English dictionaries (Doke, Malcolm, Sikakana, Vilakazi 1990); and the study by L. J. Louwrens (1991) of Northern Sotho grammar. The dictionary of !Xoon (TUU family, Taa branch) compiled by Traill (1994) also appeared at this time. George Poulos and Christian Msimang (1998) gave us a new reference grammar for Zulu; and the monumental three volumes of the *Greater Dictionary of Xhosa,* which was many years in the making, steadily appeared between 1989 and 2006 (Tshabe, Shoba, Mini and others).

An exciting development of a different kind occurred in the early 1990s, with the unexpected discovery (Crawhall 2003) of about two dozen elderly people who still spoke one of the !Ui languages (TUU) of South Africa. A call for linguists to assist with its documentation drew swift responses from overseas, and the main work on this language over the next decade and a half was conducted largely by scholars from Germany and America.

The chart presented in Figure 3 is based on data extracted from Brills's *Linguistic Bibliography*, and gives a picture of linguistic publications from **South Africa** over the past three decades. While it is not possible to make a direct comparison with the linguistic output of the immediately preceding decades, certainly the overall number of publications is cause for some celebration; and it is particularly gratifying that work on SA Sign language reflects a steady uptick throughout the three decades shown.

At the same time, sheer quantity of publications is by no means the only or even necessarily the best indicator of the health of a field. Departments of linguistics remain marginalised at most universities throughout South Africa today, and most are underfunded and understaffed. Why linguistics should have this status is not clear, but it may in part reflect a global trend.[25] The genuine

---

25   The period of South Africa's transition to the post-apartheid era coincided
       with the worldwide economic recession of 1990 to 1991, while the middle
       decade of the new era coincided with a second great recession from 2007
       to 2009. South African universities responded to these economic crises

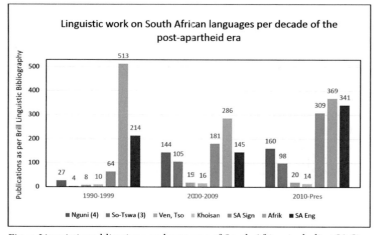

Fig. 3. Linguistic publications on languages of South Africa, including SA Sign language, for each decade of the post-apartheid period. (Figures used to draw the chart were extracted from the *Linguistic Bibliography*.) Note that Venda and Tsonga are grouped together not because of any particularly close relationship, but purely because they both have relatively few speaker numbers. For purposes of this chart, the term 'Khoisan' covers only South African Khoisan languages – effectively Khoekhoe varieties of the KHOE family, and Nǀuu, from the ǃUi branch of the TUU family. There is a minor dip in academic output in the middle decade of this period, but this may simply reflect natural fluctuation – if it was not a response to the economic recession of the same period.

struggle of linguistics departments to survive may at least partly explain the most worrisome aspect of the publications profile charted in Figure 3 – namely,

by imitating the managerialist approaches adopted by academic institutions elsewhere in the world. It was suddenly demanded of academics that they should prove their worth by pushing up their publications rate, even if this meant sacrificing quality; while departments with low student enrolments (which typically included departments of linguistics) found themselves in the firing line, and if they could not adapt expediently – for example, by devising offerings with greater mass appeal – faced incorporation into other departments, or attrition of their already few posts.

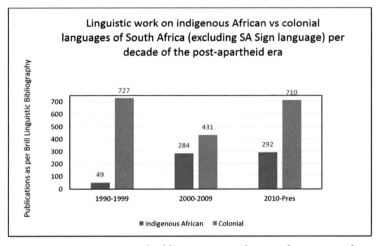

Fig. 4. Comparison in terms of publications output between linguistic work on languages of African origin and post-colonial languages of South Africa. For purposes of this chart, only work on Khoisan languages of South Africa is included in the columns for indigenous African languages – effectively Khoekhoe varieties of the KHOE family, and Nǀuu, from the !Ui branch of the TUU family. (Figures used to draw the chart were extracted from the *Linguistic Bibliography*.)

the stark disparity between linguistic work on the two post-colonial languages, and work on the nine official languages of African origin. This imbalance – the first of three that are noticed in this overview – is depicted more clearly in Figure 4.

To put it bluntly, what seems to have occurred is the persistence of an old order that privileged the study, on the part of largely white academics, of the two post-colonial languages.

This is not at all to disparage the work that focuses on varieties of South African English and Afrikaans. These are by no means exclusively 'white' languages, and some of the studies in fact examine precisely the complex issues of social identity that can arise as a consequence. The linguistic work on these languages reflects a range of contemporary approaches, and is sometimes even at the leading edge of particular theoretical frameworks, such as generative syntax. The fact that English and Afrikaans are both West Germanic languages also means that there is greater scope for international collaboration, which further enhances the quality and reach of some of this work. Most emphatically, no-one would want to wish any of this away. On the other hand, equally, there are most certainly examples of fine recent work on local African languages – some of it produced by linguists who are themselves speakers of indigenous African languages. The issue is simply that there is so much less of the latter.

The reasons for this imbalance are no doubt complex, but surely include the reality that departments of African languages at South African universities (with Unisa a notable exception) continue to focus – just as they did during the apartheid era – on only one or two languages, and continue to be understaffed,[26] with faculty being tasked mainly with teaching the languages in question, along with their associated literatures.

With the cessation of the Border War in 1990, the door was suddenly opened for many more linguists to return to areas of southern Africa that had been largely inaccessible for many decades. A number of foreign scholars were quick to take advantage of the opportunity, and the Khoisan languages rapidly became a particular focus of renewed attention. The resulting steady surge in publications is reflected in Figure 5.

One aspect of the Khoisan work not directly evident from the chart is the predominance of authorship by linguists from overseas countries as opposed to Namibia or South Africa. This is a second worrying imbalance in the overall picture of contemporary South African linguistics,[27] and seems in part to reflect the general contraction of local scholarly interest in countries beyond South Africa itself.

---

26   It is not unusual, even at some of the country's leading universities, to find a department for a single European language that has a larger complement of faculty than the department for the languages of an entire continent.

27   There is nothing wrong with having so many foreign linguists working in this particular sub-field: quite to the contrary, international collaboration is always greatly to be desired. In a field as small as this one, however, differences between foreign and local linguists in respect of mindset and historical awareness may lead to irreconcilable differences of approach that inhibit rather than promote international collaboration.

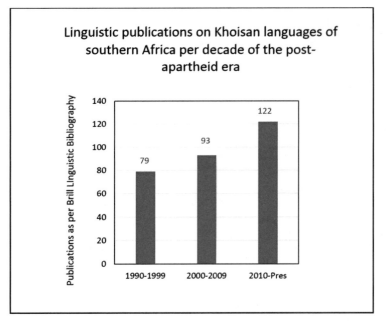

Fig. 5. Growth in the number of linguistic publications on Khoisan languages throughout southern Africa since the end of the apartheid era. The figures used to draw this chart have been extracted from the *Linguistic Bibliography*, and reflect work carried out for the most part by foreign scholars, although the chart does not indicate this specifically.

Trending themes

Work in South African linguistics over the past decade reflects a wide range of academic pre-occupations and approaches, where some are emerging, and others reflect the rapid development and expansion of established areas of research. As far as research preoccupations are concerned, one that stands out, and has already been commented on, is the burgeoning field of SA Sign language research. Most of the currently dominant themes, however, emerge almost inevitably from the multilingual character of the South African linguistic landscape, and for the most part build on foundations laid down in a previous era. The languages investigated are in many cases still only local, but are slowly beginning once again to include languages spoken by people from neighbouring countries.

One of the broad themes that emerges from the characteristic multilingualism of the country concerns aspects of language acquisition. A *psycholinguistic* approach is typically adopted in studies that focus on aspects of acquisition in bilingual or multilingual environments, where this can include natural acquisition in early childhood, as well as formal or informal secondary acquisition both at school and later on in adulthood. Ongoing attention is also being paid to aspects of language in education, such as the complexities of the multilingual classroom, the role of the child's mother tongue in early learning, and best strategies for the introduction of a second language intended to be used as the primary language of learning.

In the context of education, work in psycholinguistics and *applied linguistics* has taken on a grave urgency, with the alarming findings of a recent international survey that 78 per cent of Grade 4 children in South Africa cannot read for meaning in *any* language, including their own mother tongue, where the South African results were the lowest out of 50 countries surveyed (Spaull 2017).[28] Recently presented preliminary evidence (Spaull, Pretorius and Mohohlwane 2018) suggests that the disjunctive system of writing used for the Sotho-Tswana languages may be a factor contributing to the slow acquisition of reading skills.

A further factor contributing to the problem (apart from the poor training of teachers) is the general lack of a reading culture in most sectors of South African society. This is in no small part because of the lack of a wide range of appealing reading material, including books for children, in languages other than English an Afrikaans (Aitchison 2018).[29] The equal development of all South African languages is viewed as a national priority,[30] and a number of research chairs

---

28　"The unfolding reading crisis: the new PIRLS 2016 results," commentary published online, December 5 2017, at: https://nicspaull.com/2017/12/05/the-unfolding-reading-crisis-the-new-pirls-2016-results/.

29　"South Africa's reading crisis is a cognitive catastrophe," commentary published online, February 26 2018, at: https://theconversation.com/south-africas-reading-crisis-is-a-cognitive-catastrophe-89052.

30　The Pan-South African Language Board (PANSALB) is constitutionally mandated to oversee the equal development of all South African languages.

have recently been endowed, in the hope that ways will be found to foster this.[31] Until more original material is produced, there is a world of literature waiting to be translated, and a welcome initiative over the past few decades has been the inauguration at several universities of postgraduate programs in *translation studies*. Equally helpful has been the publication of new dictionaries, some of them intended specifically for use in schools, such as the *Oxford Bilingual School Dictionaries* series published between 2007 and 2014 for each of the South African languages. These have been prepared by *lexicographic units* based at universities around the country. (The African Association for Lexicography (Afrilex), which was established in 1995, publishes *Lexikos*, an open access (free to read) journal.)[32]

It is difficult, however – even without undertaking a formal bibliometric analysis – not to form an impression that current research interests in South African linguistics overwhelmingly reflect a *sociolinguistic* bias. This focus is brought to bear on such topics as the negotiation of multilingual environments, whether in a permanent neighbourhood or at a border crossing; or whether in the workplace,[33] at a hospital or clinic, or even in a court of law. Attention is also commonly given to the broad theme of language and identity, sometimes in sociophonetic studies of accent and class, but particularly in studies of new and often ephemeral urban varieties, such as Sepitori (Pretoria Sotho or Tswana) and Isicamtho, which feature agile code-switching, and are perhaps most often used as a kind of insider register by members of a young and 'hip' generation. Possible contact effects and the influence on these varieties of more recent immigrants is another area of investigation.

---

31   It would be remiss not to mention that the national broadcaster provides programming in all South African languages, for both radio and television. One of the informal ways in which the country's indigenous languages are being promoted is through the popular 'soaps', which not uncommonly reflect spontaneous (character-appropriate) switching between two or three different languages. Popular music also plays a role.

32   *Lexikos* is found at: http://lexikos.journals.ac.za/pub.

33   The Zulu-lexified pidgin known as Fanakolo was at one time used on South African mines at the insistence of white bosses who were unable to cope with the diversity of languages spoken by the workers. Its use was always considered demeaning, and it has now been phased out (*Chamber of Mines Annual Report 2011*: 72).

The issue of identity is also addressed in current studies of Afrikaaps, a variety of Cape Afrikaans similarly characterised by code-switching. It is possible, however, that the latter falls rather into the spectrum of Afrikaans dialects and that this kind of research effectively comes under the heading of *dialectology* or variation studies. The recognition of different varieties of Afrikaans goes back several decades (Van Rensburg 1983), but is an area of study that continues to grow. Hans den Besten (2012) contributed pioneering work in which he postulated the existence of an early Cape Pidgin, some form of which he believed could have contributed to the development of Afrikaans. Research continues into the possible substrate role of Cape Khoekhoe languages in the emergence of Afrikaans.

Work on varieties of the African languages spoken in southern Africa has a long history. For example, Doke's report (1931) on the *Unification of the Shona Dialects* necessarily included discussion of the numerous dialects constituting each of the six languages (Korekore, Zezuru, Karanga, Manyika, Ndau, Kalanga) that ideally needed to be reconciled for the creation of a standardised 'Shona language'. D. F. van der Merwe and Isaac Schapera (1943) contributed a comparative study of Kgalagadi, and Kwena and other dialects of Tswana; while Cole (1955: xv–xx) supplied further information about the Tswana dialects. Philippus van Dyk (1960) presented a dissertation on the Nguni dialect, Lala; while Ngubane (1992) presented one on another Nguni dialect, the Tembe-Thonga of KwaZulu-Natal. Simon Donnelly (2007) gave us a dissertation on Phuthi, which is evidently a variety of Nguni that has undergone extensive Sotho influence. Useful discussion of the subject is included in an overview of the Bantu languages by Robert Herbert and Richard Bailey (2002).

Another class of varieties previously much studied in South Africa was associated with members of certain social tiers, and could involve the use of lexical substitutions as well as alterations in syntax (Kunene 1971: 144, fn 2). Special registers (or 'auxiliary codes') of this kind were in fact once widely used throughout much of older Africa (Storch 2011). In South Africa, the term for the custom as formerly observed by wives or young male initiates meant 'to show respect' (Zulu *ukuhlonipha* and Sotho *ho hlonepha*). Similar codes were used, however, by a range of other groups, such as hunters, herbalists, soldiers or courtiers. The waning use of such registers in modern South Africa (Finlayson 2004) probably accounts for a corresponding decline in research on the topic.

Insights arrrived at from studies of synchronic variation as well as the effects of contact and other social phenomena (including the use of auxiliary codes) undoubtedly have the capacity to add depth and a texture of realism to diachronic studies. This makes it regrettable that the emerging field of sociohistorical linguistics so seldom features as an area of current research interest in South African linguistics.[34]

There are certainly some fine South African scholars working on core aspects of *fundamental linguistic description*. Their work is typically presented during the annual South African Microlinguistics Workshops (SAMWOP), and is often later published in *Stellenbosch Papers in Linguistics* (*SPIL*).[35] Unfortunately, these linguists constitute a rather small minority, while those who are applying such approaches to African languages, as opposed to post-colonial ones, form an even smaller sub-set. A further worrisome detail that may not be immediately apparent, but which becomes evident on a closer look at the literature itself, is that much of the leading edge research – such as work that uses a generative framework to investigate aspects of the syntax of an African language – has not been contributed by South African linguists at all, but rather by foreign scholars.

The overall disproportion in the distribution of research effort is the third imbalance observed in this overview. In short, there appears – at least on the face of things – to be an unduly great emphasis placed on sociolinguistics,[36] with rather less emphasis on psycholinguistics, and still less on the fundamentals of linguistic description. Diminished attention to core aspects of descriptive linguistics may well be another factor playing into the decline of capacity that has largely excluded South African linguists from playing their part in efforts to document the numerous minority and threatened languages of southern Africa. (Much like sociohistorical linguistics, the specialised branch of documentary linguistics is effectively non-existent in South Africa today.)

When it comes to entirely new approaches, it is safe to say that most reflect the possibilities steadily opening up for linguistics in the digital age. Locally developed *lexicographic software* such as TshwaneLex,[37] for example, has been

---

34   This branch of linguistics has much to offer to scholars from entirely different fields, such as history and archaeology. South African historians show regrettably little inclination to take advantage of this, however.

35   *SPIL* is published online (http://spil.journals.ac.za/pub) and is fully open access (free to publish, free to read).

36   No-one would want to do away altogether with the sociolinguistic work, which has the capacity to reward us with occasionally rich insights into the complexities of current social dynamics.

37   The TshwaneLex software was developed by David Joffe and Gilles-Maurice de Schryver.

used in the compilation of some of the dictionaries mentioned earlier; while scholars working in the domain of *computational linguistics* are developing software with the capacity to recognise local languages, as well as automatically parse and translate them. Digital databases of tagged and searchable corpora have already begun to serve as the basis for research; and it is likely that social media and messaging platforms will increasingly be mined for data on the range of languages, varieties, registers, and shorthand conventions used by South Africans in different contexts.

The establishment of electronic data repositories at universities around the country has been identified as a national priority, and, in a most welcome development, a repository specifically for the storage of language data (SADiLAR) has now been created at North- West University. Those linguists (almost all of them foreign) who have been working to document threatened and minority languages in southern Africa have long been in search of an acceptable regional archive for their data. The new repository is a possible solution, even though it was envisaged as a home for linguistic corpora, and is not primarily designed to function as an archive.[38] Fortunately, the linguists engaged in setting up SADiLAR have been open to communications and suggestions, so that it may yet come to serve as a greatly needed archive for endangered languages of the southern African region.

Conclusion

While South African linguistics has been slow to recover from the general crimping that occurred during the apartheid era, there have nevertheless been some encouraging and even exciting developments, particularly in the areas of research focusing on local sign languages, and computational linguistics. Three troubling imbalances have been observed, however, in the course of this overview. Recapitulated, they are:

- The stark disparity between the amount of linguistic work on the two post-colonial languages, and work on the nine official languages of African origin
- The near absence of recent work by local (as opposed to foreign) linguists on languages of the broader southern African region, and Khoisan languages in particular

---

38   It is also not specifically structured to accommodate the kinds of access (or restrictions) that may be required by communities; and in addition is currently limited to the official languages of South Africa.

- The unduly great emphasis seemingly placed on sociolinguistics, and the lesser emphasis placed on psycholinguistics and applied linguistics, as well as core aspects of fundamental descriptive linguistics

Linguistics is of course a 'broad church', and it is unwise to place too much emphasis on one branch of the field at the expense of others. Psycholinguistics and applied linguistics undoubtedly have a key role to play in the continuing reconstruction of the country, for example in helping to address the dire crisis in South African education. Given the urgency, there is at good reason to hope that more funding will be channelled in future to those researchers engaged in this critical work.[39]

It is also encouraging to note that since about 2010, the different professional bodies have increasingly held joint conferences, while in a further welcome development, early in 2018, the LSSA and SAALA were merged. The draft constitution[40] of the amalgamated body defines the association's field of focus as the 'promotion and co-ordination of the research, study and teaching, in southern Africa, of linguistics, applied linguistics, and applied language studies.' The statement of objectives includes the following:

> Bearing in mind the historical legacies of apartheid and colonialism in southern Africa, to promote transformation of the Society and its area of focus at least in terms of research, curriculum, practice and range of languages covered, in ways which promote equity of participation and access, strengthen the linguistic disciplines and empower practitioners, researchers, teachers and learners of these disciplines to develop tools to explore the full range of linguistic environments that they find themselves in.

Lastly, one of the new research chairs mentioned earlier is at Rhodes University, and it was from the African Language Studies Section in the School of Languages and Literatures at that university that the equally encouraging impetus came

---

39　It was found during the 2011 census (*Census in Brief*: 48) that, of about 31 million South Africans aged 20 years and older, more than 10 million had only 'some secondary level' schooling, while another 6,5 million had either 'some primary' or no schooling at all. Only 8,8 million had completed secondary school.

40　At April 2018 the draft document was still open for comment and had yet to be ratified.

for CLASA 2017, or the Conference of the Language Associations of Southern Africa, which constituted a joint gathering of all the professional bodies. Since indabas of this kind typically attract colleagues from neighbouring countries, the promise exists that South African linguists will in future enter more and more into transfrontier collaborations, and will return to work once again on languages of the greater southern region of Africa, with renewed attention to languages of African origin.

References

Barnard, Alan. 1985. *Nharo Wordlist*. (Department of African Languages Occasional Publications No. 2.) Durban: University of Natal.

Baumbach, E. J. M. 1987. *Analytical Tsonga Grammar*. Pretoria: Unisa Press.

Bleek, Wilhelm H. G. 1862. *A Comparative Grammar of South African Languages*, Pt 1. London: Trübner & Co.

Bleek, Dorothea. 1927. "The distribution of Bushman languages in South Africa," in *Festschrift Meinhof* (Hamburg: Augustin), 55–64.

Chebanne, Andy Monthusi. 2008. "A sociolinguistic perspective of the indigenous communities of Botswana," *African Study Monographs* 29(3): 93–118.

Cole, Desmond T. 1955. *An Introduction to Tswana Grammar*. Cape Town: Longman.

Cole, Desmond T. 1960. "African linguistic studies, 1943-1961," *African Studies* 19(4): 219–229.

Cole, Desmond T. 1971. "The history of African linguistics to 1945," in Thomas Sebeok (Ed.), *Linguistics in Sub-Saharan Africa* (Current trends in linguistics Vol 7) (The Hague: Mouton), 1–29.

Crawhall, Nigel. 2003. "The rediscovery of ǀNuu and the ǂKhomani land claim process, South Africa," in Joe Blythe and R. McKenna Brown (Eds), *Maintaining the Links: Language, identity and the land: Proceedings of the Seventh Foundation for Endangered Languages Conference* (Bristol: Foundation for Endangered Languages), 13–19.

Den Besten, Hans (Ed. Ton van den Wouden). 2012. *Roots of Afrikaans: Selected writings of Hans den Besten*. Amsterdam: John Benjamins.

Doke, Clement M. 1931. *Report on the Unification of the Shona Dialects*. Hertford: Stephen Austin and Sons.

Doke, Clement M. 1945. *Bantu: Modern grammatical, phonetical, and lexicographical studies since 1860*. London: International African Institute.

Doke, Clement M. 1961a. "The earliest records of Bantu," in Clement M Doke and Desmond Cole (Eds), *Contributions to the History of Bantu Linguistics* (Johannesburg: Wits Press), 1–7.

Doke, Clement M. 1961b. "Bantu language pioneers of the nineteenth century," in Doke and Cole (Eds), 27–53.

Doke, Clement M., D. M. Malcolm, J. M. A. Sikakana and B. W. Vilakazi. 1990. *English–Zulu, Zulu–English Dictionary*. Johannesburg: Wits University Press.

Donnelly, Simon. 2007. "Aspects of Tone and Voice in Phuthi." Urbana-Champaign: University of Illinois, PhD Thesis.

Finlayson, Rosalie. 2004. "Language and culture in South Africa," in Andries W. Oliphant, Peter Delius and Lalou Meltzer (Eds), *Democracy X: Marking the present, re-presenting the past* (Pretoria: Unisa Press), 219–231.

Greenberg, Marc L. 2015. "Introduction," in Sijmen Tol and René Genis (Eds), *Bibliography of Slavic linguistics 2000-2014. Vol. I-III* (Leiden: Brill), xxv-xxxviii. Available at: http://bibliographies.brillonline.com/browse/ bibliography-of-slavic-linguistics

Güldemann, Tom. 2004a. "TUU – a new name for the Southern Khoisan family." Leipzig: University of Leipzig, Institut für Afrikanistik.

Güldemann, Tom. 2004b. "Reconstruction through 'deconstruction': the marking of person, gender, and number in the Khoe family and Kwadi," *Diachronica* 21(2): 251–306.

Güldemann, Tom and Rainer Vossen. 2000. "Khoisan," in Bernd Heine and Derek Nurse (Eds), *African Languages: an introduction* (Cambridge: CUP), 99–122.

Heine, Bernd and Henry Honken. 2010. "The Kx'a Family: a new Khoisan genealogy," *Journal of Asian and African Studies* 79: 5–36.

Herbert, Robert K. and Richard Bailey. 2002. "The Bantu languages: sociohistorical perspectives," in Rajend Mesthrie (Ed.), *Language in South Africa* (Cambridge: CUP), 50–78.

Kunene, Daniel. 1971. *Heroic Poetry of the Basotho*. Oxford: OUP.

Lanham, L. W. 1978. "An outline history of the languages of southern Africa," in L. W. Lanham and K. P. Prinsloo (Eds), *Language and Communication Studies in South Africa* (Cape Town: OUP), 13–28.

Linguistic Bibliography. Available at: www.linguisticbibliography.com [Consulted in March 2018].

Louw, J. A. and J. B. Jubase. 1978. *Handboek van Xhosa*. Johannesburg: Educum.

Louwrens, L. J. 1991. *Aspects of Northern Sotho Grammar*. Pretoria: Via Afrika.

Mabille, Adolphe and H. Dieterlin (Rev. R. A. Paroz). 1961. *Southern Sotho–English Dictionary (South African orthography)*. Morija: Morija Sesuto Book Depot.

Maho, Jouni. 2009. *NUGL Online: The online version of the New Updated Guthrie List, a referential classification of the Bantu languages*. Available at: https://

brill.com/fileasset/downloads_products/35125_Bantu-New-updated-Guthrie-List.pdf.

McLaren, J (rev. W. G. Bennie and J. J. R. Jolobe). 1963. *A New Concise Xhosa–English Dictionary.* Cape Town: Longmans Southern Africa.

Mesthrie, Rajend. 2002. "South Africa: a sociolinguistic overview," in Mesthrie (Ed.), *Language in South Africa* (Cambridge: CUP), 11–26.

Ngubane, Sihawukele. 1992. "The Northern Zululand dialects." Durban: University of Natal, MA Thesis.

Nienaber, Gabriel S. 1989. *Khoekhoense Stamname: 'n voorlopige verkenning.* Pretoria, Cape Town: Academica,

Nienaber, Gabriel S, and P. E. Raper. 1977, 1980. *Toponymica Hottentotica* (3 vols). Pretoria: Human Sciences Research Council.

Poulos, George. 1990. *A Linguistic Analysis of Venda.* Pretoria: Via Afrika.

Poulos, George and Christian Msimang. 1998. *A Linguistic Analysis of Zulu.* Cape Town: Via Afrika.

Rycroft, D. K. 1981. *Concise SiSwati Dictionary.* Pretoria: Van Schaik Publishers.

Snyman, Jan. 1970. *An Introduction to the !Xũ (!Kung) language.* (Communication of the UCT School of African Studies.) Cape Town: A. A. Balkema.

Snyman, Jan. c. 1975. *Zul'hõasi Fonologie en Woordeboek.* Cape Town: A. A. Balkema.

Spaull, Nic, E. Pretorius and N. Mohohlwane. 2018. "Investigating the comprehension iceberg: developing empirical benchmarks for early grade reading in agglutinating African languages." RESEP Working Paper Series No. WP01/2018, available at: (http://resep.sun.ac.za/index.php/research-outputs/stellenbosch-working-paers/2018-2/).

Storch, Anne. 2011. *Secret Manipulations: Language and context in Africa.* Oxford: OUP.

Tshabe, Sonwabo Lungile, F. M. Shoba, Buyiswa Mavis Mini, H. W. Pahl, A. M. Pienaar, and T. A. Ndungane. 2006. *The Greater Dictionary of IsiXhosa* (3 vols). Alice: University of Fort Hare.

Traill, Anthony. 1985. *Phonetic and Phonological Studies of !XOO Bushman.* Hamburg: Helmut Buske.

Traill, Anthony. 1994. *A !Xóõ Dictionary.* Cologne: Rüdiger Köppe.

Van der Merwe, D. F. and Isaac Schapera. 1943. "A comparative study of Kgalagadi, Kwena and other Sotho dialects." (Communication of the UCT School of African Studies.) Cape Town: UCT.

Van Dyk, Philippus. 1960. "'n Studie van Lala: Sy fonologie, morfologie en sintaksis." Stellenbosch: Stellenbosch University, PhD Thesis.

Van Rensburg, M. C. J. 1983. "Nie-standaardvorme, variasiepatrone en Afrikaans uit die vorige eeu," in G. N. Claassen and M. C. J. van Rensburg (Eds),

Taalverskeidenheid: 'n blik op die spektrum van taalvariasie in Afrikaans (Pretoria, Cape Town: Academica), 134–161.

Vossen, Rainer. 1997. *Die Khoe-Sprachen: Ein Beitrag zur Erforschung der Sprachgeschichte Afrikas.* Cologne: Rüdiger Köppe.

Westphal, Ernst O. J. 1963. "The linguistic prehistory of southern Africa: Bush, Kwadi, Hottentot and Bantu linguistic relationships," *Africa* 33: 237–265.

Witzlack-Makarevich, Alena. 2006. "Aspects of Information Structure in Richtersveld Nama." Leipzig: University of Leipzig, MA Thesis.

Ziervogel, Dirk and Enos John Mabuza. 1976. *A Grammar of the Swati Language.* Pretoria: Van Schaik.

STRUCTURE OF REFERENCES

Books

1. Monographs

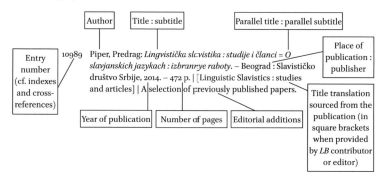

Author

Title : subtitle

Parallel title : parallel subtitle

Entry number (cf. indexes and cross-references)

10989 Piper, Predrag: *Lingvistička slavistika : studije i članci = O slavjanskich jazykach : izbranrye raboty.* – Beograd : Slavističko društvo Srbije, 2014. – 472 p. | [Linguistic Slavistics : studies and articles] | A selection of previously published papers.

Place of publication : publisher

Year of publication

Number of pages

Editorial additions

Title translation sourced from the publication (in square brackets when provided by *LB* contributor or editor)

2. Edited volumes

Title

Editorial responsibilities (*verbatim* title page)

1st place of publication : publisher

120 *Germanistische Linguistik extra muros : Aufgaben* / Hrsg. von Iwona Bartoszewicz ; Martine Dalmas ; Joanna Szczęk ; Artur Tworek. – Wrocław : Oficyna Wyd. ATUT – Wrocławskie Wyd. Oświatowe ; Dresden : Neisse, 2009. – 231 p. – (*OrbL* ; Beiheft 85) ; (Linguistische Treffen in Wrocław ; 4) | Proceedings of a conference held in Wrocław, September 2008

1st series title ; number in series

2nd place of publication : publisher

Editorial additions

2nd series title ; number in series

Year of publication

Number of pages

STRUCTURE OF REFERENCES

Articles

1. In a periodical

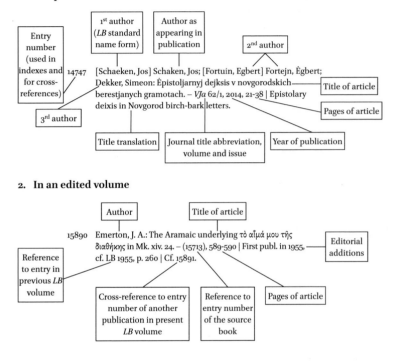

2. In an edited volume

PERIODICALS

This list contains the full titles and abbreviations of periodicals used in this volume. The complete list of periodicals covered in the *Linguistic Bibliography* may be consulted at http://bibliographies.brillonline.com/pages/lb/periodicals.

AUW	Acta Universitatis Wratislaviensis. Wrocław. ISSN: 0239-6661.
EWW	English world-wide : a journal of varieties of English. Amsterdam. ISSN: 0172-8865. eISSN: 1569-9730.
FL	Functions of language. Amsterdam. ISSN: 0929-998X. eISSN: 1569-9765.
FLang	First language. London. ISSN: 0142-7237. eISSN: 1740-2344.
Glossa	Glossa : a journal of general linguistics. eISSN: 2397-1835.
IJSL	International journal of the sociology of language. Berlin. ISSN: 0165-2516. eISSN: 1613-3668.
IN	Internationale Neerlandistiek. Amsterdam. ISSN: 1876-9071. eISSN: 2214-5729.
Interspeech	Interspeech. S. l. ISSN: 1990-9772.
IPRG	Intercultural pragmatics. Berlin. ISSN: 1612-295X. eISSN: 1613-365X.
JASA	The journal of the Acoustical Society of America. Melville, NY.
JChL	Journal of child language. Cambridge. ISSN: 0305-0009. eISSN: 1469-7602.
JGL-SGL	Journal of Germanic linguistics. Cambridge. ISSN: 1470-5427. eISSN: 1475-3014.
JPCL	Journal of pidgin and creole languages. Amsterdam. ISSN: 0920-9034. eISSN: 1569-9870.
Language	Language : journal of the Linguistic Society of America. Baltimore, MD. ISSN: 0097-8507. eISSN: 1535-0665.
Lexikos	Lexikos. Stellenbosch. ISSN: 1684-4904. eISSN: 2224-0039.
LgDC	Language dynamics and change. Leiden. ISSN: 2210-5824. eISSN: 2210-5832.
LIN	Linguistics in the Netherlands : AVT publications. Amsterdam. ISSN: 0929-7332. eISSN: 1569-9919.

PERIODICALS

Linguistics	Linguistics : an interdisciplinary journal of the language sciences. Berlin. ISSN: 0024-3949. eISSN: 1613-396X.
LiS	Language in society. Cambridge. ISSN: 0047-4045.
Literator	Literator : journal of literary criticism, comparative linguistics and literary studies = tysdkrif vir besondere en vergelykende taal- en literatuurstudie. Cape Town. ISSN: 0258-2279. eISSN: 2219-8237.
LLACAN	Linguistique et langues africaines revue scientifique du Llacan. Paris. ISSN: 2429-2230.
LM	Language matters : studies in the languages of Africa. London. ISSN: 1022-8195. eISSN: 1753-5395.
LPLP	Language problems and language planning. Amsterdam. ISSN: 0272-2690. eISSN: 1569-9889.
LRE	Language resources and evaluation. Dordrecht. ISSN: 1574-020X. eISSN: 1574-0218.
Multiling	Multilingual margins : a journal of multilingualism from the periphery. S. l. eISSN: 2221-4216.
NAfr	Nomina africana : journal of the Names Society of Southern Africa = Tydskrif van die Naamkundevereniging van Suider-Afrika. Durban. ISSN: 1012-0254. eISSN: 2070-2639.
NeerlW	NeerlandicaWratislaviensia.Wroclaw. ISSN: 0860-0716.
NJAS	Nordic journal of African studies. Helsinki. ISSN: 1235-4481. eISSN: 1459-9465.
PerLinguam	Per linguam : a journal for language learning = tydskrif vir taalaanleer. Stellenbosch. ISSN: 0259-2312. eISSN: 2224-0012.
SAfrJAL	South African journal of African languages = Suid-Afrikaanse tijdskrif vir Afrikatale. Pretoria. ISSN: 0257-2117. eISSN: 2305-1159.
SALALS	Southern African linguistics and applied language studies. Grahamstown. ISSN: 1607-3614. eISSN: 1727-9461.
SPIL	Stellenbosch papers in linguistics. Stellenbosch. ISSN: 1027-3417. eISSN: 2223-9936.
SPILPLUS	Stellenbosch papers in linguistics PLUS. Stellenbosch. ISSN: 1726-541X. eISSN: 2224-3380.
TNA	Tydskrif vir Nederlands en Afrikaans. Pretoria. ISSN: 1022-6966.
TsGw	Tydskrif vir geesteswetenskappe. Pretoria. ISSN: 0041-4751. eISSN: 2224-7912.

ABBREVIATIONS

The following is a list of abbreviations used in the *Bibliography of South African Languages*. Please note that wherever these abbreviations appear in the titles of publications, they were used so by the authors.

ab.	abstract	Fr.	French
Acad.	Academy	G.	German
Afr.	African	Hrsg.	Herausgeber, herausgegeben
art.	article	inst.	institute
ass.	association	introd.	introduction, introductory
biblio.	bibliography	LB	Linguistic Bibliography
cf.	confer (compare, "see")	lg.	language
ch.	chapter	ling.	linguistic, linguistics
Chin.	Chinese	n.s.	new series, nouvelle série
comm.	commentary	p	page(s)
conf.	conference	Pol.	Polish
cont.	continuation, continued	publ.	publication(s), published
contr.	contribution(s)	rev.	review
coord.	coordinator, coordinated	s.l.	sine loco (no place)
dir.	direction, directeur,	s.n.	sine nomine (no publisher)
	directrice	Sp.	Spanish
disc.	discussion	summ.	summary
diss.	dissertation	suppl.	supplement
Du.	Dutch	transl.	translation, translated,
E.	English		translator
ed.	edited, editor, edition	univ.	university
fac.	faculty		

BECOME A CONTRIBUTOR TO THE *LINGUISTIC BIBLIOGRAPHY*

The editorial team is looking for specialists who would like to contribute to the *Linguistic Bibliography* by gathering and compiling bibliographical references in their field of expertise.

The *Linguistic Bibliography*, published in annual print volumes and online, is a collection of detailed bibliographical descriptions of linguistic publications on general and language-specific theoretical linguistics. While the bibliography aims to cover all languages of the world, particular attention is given to the inclusion of publications on endangered and lesser-studied languages. Publications in any language are collected, analyzed and annotated (using a state-of-the-art system of subject and language keywords) by an international team of linguists and contributors from all over the world.

If you are interested in joining the *Linguistic Bibliography*, please contact the editors via lb@brill.com.

For more information, visit brill.com/lbcontributor or scan the QR-code below.

General works

3. Conferences, workshops, meetings

1   *Afrolusitanistik – eine vergessene Disziplin in Deutschland? : Dokumenta-*
    tion des 2. Bremer Afro-Romania Kolloquiums vom 27.-29. Juni 1996 / Ruth
    Degenhardt ; Thomas Stolz ; Hella Ulferts. – Bremen : Univ. Bremen,
    1996. – 399 p. – (Bremer Beiträge zur Afro-Romania ; 2).

2   *Akten des XII. Internationalen Germanistenkongresses, Warschau 2010 : Viel-*
    heit und Einheit der Germanistik weltweit : deutsche Morphologie im Kontrast-
    Beschreibende deutsche Grammatik- Synthetische Grammatik des Deutschen
    als einzelsprachliche Grammatik auf universeller Basis- Corpusdaten und
    grammatische Regeln- Sprachkonzepte und Grammatikmodelle im DaFiA- /
    Hrsg. von Franciszek Grucza ; Mitherausgeber: Peter Colliander, Józef Dar-
    ski, Kennosuke Ezawa, Stefan J. Schierholz, Horst J. Simon. – Frankfurt
    am Main : Peter Lang, 2012. – 389 p. – (Publikationen der Internationalen
    Vereinigung für Germanistik ; 15) | [Proceedings of the 12th International
    Germanists' Congress, Warsaw 2010 : the diversity and unity of German
    philology worldwide : German morphology in contrast – descriptive Ger-
    man grammar – synthetic grammar of German as individual grammar on a
    universal basis – corpus data and grammar rules – language concepts and
    grammar models in German as a foreign language abroad] | G. ab.

3   *The Arabic script in Africa : studies in the use of a writing system* / Ed.
    by Meikal Mumin ; Kees Versteegh. – Leiden : Brill, 2014. – xix, 400 p. –
    (Studies in Semitic languages and linguistics ; 71) | Papers based on pre-
    sentations at the TASIA (The Arabic script in Africa: diffusion, usage,
    diversity and dynamics of a writing system) workshop, held on April 6-7,
    2010, at the Univ. of Cologne, Germany.

4   *Binamn : uppkomst, bildning, terminologi och bruk : handlingar från*
    NORNA:s 40:e symposium i Älvkarleö, Uppland, 29/9-1/10 2010 / Redigerade
    av Staffan Nyström (huvudredaktör) ; Eva Brylla ; Katharina Leibring ;
    Lennart Ryman & Per Vikstrand. – Uppsala : NORNA-Förlaget, 2012. – 192
    p. – (NORNA-rapporter ; 88) | With summaries in English.

5   *Complex processes in new languages* / Ed. by Enoch Oladé Aboh ; Norval
     Smith. – Amsterdam : Benjamins, 2009. – vii, 409 p. – (Creole language
     library ; 35) | Selected papers from the Sixth Creolistics Workshop held
     in Giessen, 2006.

6   *Consonant clusters and structural complexity* / Ed. by Philip Hoole ;
     Lasse Bombien ; Marianne Pouplier ; Christine Mooshammer ; Barbara
     Kühnert. – Berlin : De Gruyter Mouton, 2012. – vi, 409 p. – (Interface
     explorations ; 26) | Selected papers from a meeting in Munich in the
     summer of 2008.

7   *Continuity and change in grammar* / Ed. by Anne Breitbarth ; Christopher
     Lucas ; Sheila Watts ; David Willis. – Amsterdam : Benjamins, 2010. – viii,
     359 p. – (Linguistik aktuell = Linguistics today ; 159) | Selected papers
     from the Continuity and change in grammar conference, Univ. of
     Cambridge, 18-20 March 2008.

8   *Cyclical change* / Ed. by Elly van Gelderen. – Amsterdam : Benjamins,
     2009. – viii, 329 p. – (Linguistik aktuell = Linguistics today ; 146) | Papers
     presented during the Workshop on the Linguistic Cycle at Arizona
     State University in April 2008.

9   *Diversity in African languages : selected papers from the 46th annual con-
     ference on African Linguistics* / Ed. by Doris L. Payne ; Sara Pacchiarotti ;
     Mokaya Bosire. – Berlin : Language science press, 2016. – vii, 589 p. –
     (Contemporary African linguistics ; 1) | Papers from the 46th Annual
     Conference on African Linguistics, University of Oregon, March 26-28,
     2015.

10 *Electronic lexicography in the 21st century : new applications for new
     users : proceedings of eLex 2011* / Ed. by Iztok Kosem and Karmen
     Kosem. – Ljubljana : Trojina, zavod za uporabno slovenistiko = institute
     for applied Slovene studies, 2011. – ix, 310 p | Proceedings of eLex, Bled,
     10-12 November 2011 | Electronic publ.

11 *Exploring linguistic standards in non-dominant varieties of pluricen-
     tric languages.Explorando estándares lingüísticos en variedades no
     dominantes de lenguas pluricéntricas* / Rudolf Muhr ; Carla Amorós
     Negre ; Carmen Fernández Juncal ; Klaus Zimmermann ; Emilio Prieto ;
     Natividad Hernández (eds.). – Frankfurt am Main : Lang, 2013. – 484 p. –
     (Österreichisches Deutsch. Sprache der Gegenwart ; 15) | E. & Sp. papers
     presented at the "2nd International conference on non-dominant vari-
     eties of pluricentric languages", held in Salamanca (Spain), 11-13 July,
     2012.

12 *FEL XX Language Colonization and Endangerment : long-term effects,
     echoes and reactions : proceedings of the 20th FEL Conference* / Editors:

Nicholas Ostler and Panchanan Mohanty. – Hungerford : Foundation for Endangered Languages, 2016. – xiv, 200 p | Conference held at Hyderabad, Centre for Endangered Languages and Mother Tongue Studies, 9 – 12 December 2016.

13 *Geographical typology and linguistic areas : with special reference to Africa* / Ed. by Osamu Hieda ; Christa König ; Hiroshi Nakagawa. – Amsterdam : Benjamins, 2011. – vi, 321 p. – (Tokyo University of Foreign Studies. Studies in linguistics ; 2).

14 *Historical linguistics 2009 : selected papers from the 19th international conference on historical linguistics, Nijmegen, 10-14 August 2009* / Ed. by Ans van Kemenade ; Nynke de Haas. – Amsterdam : Benjamins, 2012. – xxi, 404 p. – (Current issues in linguistic theory ; 320).

15 *Językoznawstwo historyczne i typologiczne : w 100-lecie urodzin Profesora Tadeusza Milewskiego* / Komitet red. Leszek Bednarczuk ; Wojciech Smoczyński ; Maria Wojtyła-Świerzowska. – Kraków : Polska Akad. Umiejętności, 2008. – 708 p. – (Rozprawy Wydziału Filologicznego ; 76) | Contributions to a conference 'Historical and typological linguistics' held in Cracow, 12-13 Dec. 2006, on the occasion of the 100th birthday of Tadeusz Milewski (1906-1966).

16 *Khoisan languages and linguistics : proceedings of the 5th International Symposium, July 13-17, 2014, Riezlern/Kleinwalsertal* / Sheena Shah ; Mattias Brenzinger (eds.). – Köln : Köppe, 2016. – 362 p. – (Quellen zur Khoisan-Forschung = Research in Khoisan studies ; 34).

17 *Linguistic complexity : second language acquisition, indigenization, contact* / Ed. by Bernd Kortmann ; Benedikt Szmrecsanyi. – Berlin, Boston : De Gruyter, 2012. – vi, 264 p. – (Linguae & litterae ; 13) | Papers from a workshop held at the Freiburg Institute for Advanced Studies (FRIAS) in May 2009.

18 *Monosyllables : from phonology to typology* / Thomas Stolz ; Nicole Nau ; Cornelia Stroh (eds.). – Berlin : Akademie Verlag, 2012. – 248 p. – (Studia typologica. Beihefte zu Sprachtypologie und Universalienforschung ; 12) | Papers from an international conference held in Bremen, 28-30 October, 2009, as part of the program of the *Festival of languages*.

19 *Multilingual individuals and multilingual societies* / Ed. by Kurt Braunmüller and Christoph Gabriel. – Amsterdam : Benjamins, 2012. – xiii, 474 p. – (Hamburg studies on multilingualism ; 13) | Selected papers from an international conference held in Hamburg (October 2010).

20 *Philologia Frisica anno 2008 : lêzings fan it achttjinde Frysk Filologekongres fan de Fryske Akademy op 10, 11 en 12 desimber 2008* / Kongreskommisje/redaksje: P. Boersma ; G. Th. Jensma ; R. Salverda. –

Ljouwert = Leeuwarden : Fryske Akademy, 2012. – 298 p | Frisian, G., Du. & E. text.

21 *Proceedings of the 10th LASU Conference, Roma, Lesotho, 25-27 November 2009 : language contact, identity and socio-economic mobility* / edited by Alison Love, 'Mulillo Machobane, Francina Moloi, Thekiso Khati, Beatrice Ekanjume & Taclo Qhala. – [Maseru] : National University of Lesotho, 2011. – viii, 441 p.

22 *Proceedings of the 29th West Coast Conference on Formal Linguistics* / ed. by Jaehoon Choi, E. Alan Hogue, Jeffrey Punske, Deniz Tat, Jessamyn Schertz, and Alex Trueman. – Somerville, MA : Cascadilla, 2012. – viii, 406 p. – (West Coast Conference on Formal Linguistics ; 29) | Conference took place April 22-24, 2011 at University of Arizona.

23 *Proceedings of the 33rd West Coast Conference on Formal Linguistics* / ed. by Kyeong-min Kim, Pocholo Umbal, Trevor Block, Queenie Chan, Tanie Cheng, Kelli Finney, Mara Katz, Sophie Nickel-Thompson, and Lisa Shorten. – Somerville, MA : Cascadilla, 2016. – viii, 426 p. – (West Coast Conference on Formal Linguistics ; 33) | Conference took place March 27-29, 2015 at Simon Fraser University.

24 *Proceedings of the thirty-fourth annual meeting of the Berkeley Linguistics Society, February 8-10, 2008 : general session and parasession on information structure.* – *BLS* / Ed. by Sarah Berson, Alex Bratkievich, Daniel Bruhn, Amy Campbell, Ramon Escamilla, Allegra Giovine, Lindsey Newbold, Marilola Perez, Marta Piqueras-Brunet, Russell Rhomieux. – Berkeley, CA : Berkeley Linguistics Society, 2012. – iii, 482 p. – *(BLS* ; 34).

25 *Proceedings of the 34th West Coast Conference on Formal Linguistics* / ed. by Aaron Kaplan, Abby Kaplan, Miranda K. McCarvel, and Edward J. Rubin. – Somerville, MA : Cascadilla, 2017. – vii, 598 p. – (West Coast Conference on Formal Linguistics ; 34) | Conference took place April 29-May 1, 2016 at the University of Utah.

26 *Proceedings of the thirty-seventh annual meeting of the Berkeley Linguistics Society, February 12-13, 2011 : general session and parasession on language, gender, and sexuality.* – *BLS* / Edited by Chundra Cathcart ; I-Hsuan Chen ; Greg Finley ; Shinae Kang ; Clare S. Sandy ; Elise Stickles. – Berkeley, CA : Berkeley Linguistics Society, 2013. – vi, 478 p. – *(BLS* ; 37).

27 *Proceedings of the First Workshop on Computational Approaches to Compound Analysis : held at the 25th International Conference on Computational Linguistics (COLING 2014)* / Editors: Ben Verhoeven ; Walter

Daelemans ; Menno van Zaanen ; Gerhard van Huyssteen. – Dublin : Dublin City University ; Stroudsburg, PA : Ass. for Computational Linguistics, 2014. – vii, 91 p.

28   *Proceedings of the 6th World Congress of African Linguistics, Cologne, 17-21 August 2009* / Ed. by Matthias Brenzinger ; Anne-Maria Fehn. – Köln : Köppe, 2012. – xiv, 658 p.

29   *Prosodic categories : production, perception and comprehension* / Ed. by Sónia Frota ; Gorka Elordieta ; Pilar Prieto. – Dordrecht : Springer, 2011. – viii, 296 p. – (Studies in natural language and linguistic theory ; 82) | Papers from the Third Tone and Intonation in Europe Conference (TIE3), held in Lisbon, September 2008.

30   *Selected proceedings of the 40th annual conference on African linguistics : African languages and linguistics today* / Ed. by Eyamba G. Bokamba ; Ryan K. Shosted ; Bezza Tesfaw Ayalew. – Somerville, MA : Cascadilla Proceedings Project, 2011. – viii, 230 p. | Conference held at the Univ. of Illinois at Urbana-Champaign, April 9-11, 2009.

31   *Selected proceedings of the 43rd annual conference on African linguistics : linguistic interfaces in African languages* / Ed. by Ọlanikẹ Ọla Orie ; Karen W. Sanders. – Somerville, MA : Cascadilla Proceedings Project, 2013. – vi, 277 p. | Papers from a conference held at Tulane Univ., 15-17 March, 2012 | Also freely available online.

32   *Selected proceedings of the 42nd Annual conference of African linguistics : African languages in context* / Ed. by Michael R. Marlo ; Nikki B. Adams ;Christopher R. Green ; Michelle Morrison ; Tristan M. Purvis. – Somerville, MA : Cascadilla Proceedings Project, 2012. – xi, 337 p. | Free web access to articles.

33   *Standaardtalen in beweging* / Red.: Marijke J. van der Wal ; Eep Francken. – Münster : Nodus, 2010. – 217 p. | Papers from the symposium 'Standaardtalen in beweging : standaardisatie en destandaardisatie in Nederland, Vlaanderen en Zuid-Afrika', held at the Univ. of Leiden, 19-21 August 2009.

34   *Theoretical approaches to disharmonic word order* / Ed. by Theresa Biberauer ; Michelle L. Sheehan. – Oxford : Oxford UP, 2013. – xvi, 532 p. – (Oxford linguistics) | All papers but one originated from a conference held in Newcastle, 2009.

35   *Viva Africa 2008 : proceedings of the IIIrd international conference on African studies* / Ed. by Tomáš Machalík ; Jan Záhořík. – Plzeň : Západočeská univ., 2008. – 351 p.

36   *World Englishes : problems, properties and prospects : selected papers from the 13th IAWE conference* / Ed. by Thomas Hoffmann ; Lucia

Siebers. – Amsterdam : Benjamins, 2009. – xix, 436 p. – (Varieties of English around the world ; G40) | Selected papers from the 13th IAWE conference held at Regensburg University, October 2007.

4. Festschriften and miscellanies

4.1. Festschriften

37 *Gradual creolization : studies celebrating Jacques **Arends*** | Ed. by Rachel Selbach ; Hugo Cardoso ; Margot van den Berg. – Amsterdam : Benjamins, 2009. – x, 392 p. – (Creole language library ; 34).

38 *Lexicography in the 21st century : in honour of Henning **Bergenholtz*** | Ed. by Sandro Nielsen and Sven Tarp. – Amsterdam : Benjamins, 2009. – xi, 341 p. – (Terminology and lexicography research and practice ; 12).

39 *The view from Building 20 : essays in linguistics in honor of Sylvain **Bromberger*** | Ed. by Kenneth Hale ; Samuel Jay Keyser. – Cambridge, MA : MIT Press, 1993. – xi, 273 p. – (Current studies in linguistics series ; 24).

40 *African languages and linguistic theory : a festschrift in honour of Professor Herbert **Chimhundu*** | Edited by Langa Khumalo. – Cape Town : CASAS, 2014. – xiii, 297 p. – (CASAS book series ; 109).

41 *Die tand van die tyd : opstelle opgedra aan Jac **Conradie*** | Redakteurs: Willie Burger en Marné Pienaar. – Stellenbosch : Sun Press, 2009. – iii, 227 p. | [*Die tand van die tyd* : essays dedicated to Jac Conradie].

42 *Voor Magda : artikelen voor Magda **Devos** bij haar afscheid van de Universiteit Gent* | Johan De Caluwe & Jacques Van Keymeulen [red.]. – Gent : Vakgroep Nederlandse Taalkunde, Univ. Gent ; Gent : Academia Press, 2010. – 816 p.

43 *Festschrift Rufus H. **Gouws*** | Redakteurs/Editors/Éditeurs: Willem Botha ; Paul Mavoungou ; Dion Nkomo. – Stellenbosch : Sun Press, 2013. – xiv, 299 p. | Afrikaans, E. & Fr. articles.

44 *Between west and east : Festschrift for Wim **Honselaar** on the occasion of his 65th birthday* | Ed. by René Genis ; Eric de Haard ; Janneke Kalsbeek ; Evelien Keizer ; Jenny Stelleman. – Amsterdam : Pegasus, 2012. – xvi, 740 p. – (Pegasus Oost-Europese Studies ; 20).

45 *Structure preserved : studies in syntax for Jan **Koster*** | Ed. by C. Jan-Wouter Zwart ; Mark de Vries. – Amsterdam : Benjamins, 2010. – xxiii, 395 p. – (Linguistik aktuell = Linguistics today ; 164).

46 *Bantu languages and linguistics : papers in memory of Dr. Rugatiri D. K. Mekacha [1956-2001]* / Karsten Legère (ed.). – Eckersdorf : Breitinger, 2013. – ii, 314 p. – (Bayreuth African studies ; 91).

47 *In and out of Africa : languages in question in honour of Robert Nicolaï.* Vol. 1. *Language contact and epistemological issues* / Ed. by Carole de Féral. – Leuven : Peeters, 2013. – 236 p. – (Bibliothèque des cahiers de l'Institut de Linguistique de Louvain ; 130) | E. & Fr. text | Cf. 48.

48 *In and out of Africa : languages in question : in honour of Robert Nicolaï.* Vol. 2. *Language contact and language change in Africa* / Ed. by Carole de Féral ; Maarten Kossmann ; Mauro Tosco. – Louvain-la-Neuve : Peeters, 2014. – 329 p. – (Bibliothèque des cahiers de l'Institut de Linguistique de Louvain ; 132) | E. & Fr. text | Cf. 47.

49 *Social lives in language : sociolinguistics and multilingual speech communities : celebrating the work of Gillian Sankoff* / Ed. by Miriam Meyerhoff ; Naomi Nagy. – Amsterdam : Benjamins, 2008. – ix, 365 p. – (Impact. Studies in language and society ; 24).

50 *Language contact in Africa and the African diaspora in the Americas : in honor of John V. Singler* / Edited by Cecelia Cutler ; Zvjezdana Vrzić ; Philipp Angermeyer. – Amsterdam : Benjamins, 2017. – vii, 369 p. – (Creole language library ; 53).

51 *Lone Tree : scholarship in the service of the Koon : essays in memory of Anthony T Traill* / edited by Rainer Vossen & Wilfied H G Haacke. – Köln : Köppe, 2016. – 458 p.

General linguistics and related disciplines

0.2.   History of linguistics, biographical data, organizations

0.2.1.   Western traditions

0.2.1.6.   Nineteenth century

52   *Kolonialzeitliche Sprachforschung : die Beschreibung afrikanischer und ozeanischer Sprachen zur Zeit der deutschen Kolonialherrschaft* / Thomas Stolz ; Christina Vossmann ; Barbara Dewein (Hrsg.). – Berlin : Akademie Verlag, 2011. – 312 p. – (Koloniale und postkoloniale Linguistik = Colonial and postcolonial linguistics ; 1).

53   Oosthuysen, J. C. (Koos): Extricating the description of the grammar of isiXhosa from a Eurocentric approach. – *SAfrJAL* 35/1, 2015, 83-92.

54   Rensburg, Christo van: Oor die eerste 50 jaar se maak aan Standaardafrikaans = Creating a standardised version of Afrikaans : the first 50 years. – *TsGw* 55/3, 2015, 319-342 | E. & Afrikaans ab.

55   Russow, Gerald: "... die Ursache der grammatischen Zersetzung des Kapholländischen..." : der Briefwechsel zwischen Hugo Schuchardt und Nicolaas Mansvelt. – *GLS* 78, 2012, 75-99 | Hugo Schuchardt (1842-1927) | Nicolaas Mansvelt (1852-1933).

56   Swart, Corlietha: Landmeter Von Wielligh op ongekarteerde taallandskap. – *TNA* 16/2, 2009, 92-104 | [Surveyor Von Wielligh in the unchartered linguistic landscape] | E. ab.

0.2.1.7.   Twentieth century

57   Mafela, Munzhedzi James: L.T. Marole : a forgotten pioneer in Tshivenḓa lexicography. – *Lexikos* 18, 2008, 366-373 | E. & Afrikaans ab.

58   Zonneveld, Wim: Fonologie en het Afrikaans – van regels via parameters naar constraints. – *TsGw* 51/4, 2011, 730-745 | Phonology and Afrikaans – from rules to parameters to constraints.

69 *Challenging sonority : cross-linguistic evidence* / edited by Martin J. Ball and Nicole Müller. – London : Equinox, 2016. – vi, 455 p. – (Studies in phonetics and phonology).

1.1. Phonetics

1.1.1. Articulatory phonetics

70 Bateman, Nicoleta: Palatalization as overlap of articulatory gestures : crosslinguistic evidence. – (24), 25-36.

1.1.3. Auditory phonetics

71 Best, Catherine T.; Hallé, Pierre A.: Perception of initial obstruent voicing is influenced by gestural organization. – *JPhon* 38/1, 2010, 109-126 | On the perception of Zulu, Tlingit and Hebrew obstruent voicing by English and French listeners.

1.2. Phonology

72 *Phonological explorations : empirical, theoretical and diachronic issues* / Bert Botma ; Roland Noske (eds.). – Berlin : De Gruyter Mouton, 2012. – x, 355 p. – (Linguistische Arbeiten ; 548).

1.2.1. Suprasegmental phonology (prosody)

73 Kenstowicz, Michael J.: Evidence for metrical constituency. – (39), 257-273.

2. Grammar, morphosyntax

74 *On looking into words (and beyond) : structures, relations, analyses* / Ed. by Claire Bowern ; Laurence Horn ; Raffaella Zanuttini. – Berlin : Language science press, 2017. – xi, 609 p. – (Empirically oriented theoretical morphology and syntax ; 3) | A tribute to Stephen R. Anderson.

75 *Word classes : nature, typology and representations* / Ed. by Raffaele Simone ; Francesca Masini. – Amsterdam : Benjamins, 2014. – vii, 293 p. – (Current issues in linguistic theory ; 332).

2.2. Syntax

76   *Approaches to complex predicates* / Ed. by Léa Nash ; Pollet Samvelian. –
     Leiden : Brill, 2016 [2015]. – 295 p. – (Syntax & semantics ; 41).

77   *Cleft structures* / Ed. by Katharina Hartmann ; Tonjes
     Veenstra. – Amsterdam : Benjamins, 2013. – viii, 348 p. – (Linguistik
     aktuell = Linguistics today ; 208`.

78   Halpert, Claire: Raising parameters. – (23), 186-195 | E. ab.

79   *Microvariation in syntactic doubling* / Ed. by Sjef Barbiers ; Olaf
     Koeneman ; Marika Lekakou ; Margreet van der Ham. – Bingley :
     Emerald, 2008. – xiv, 479 p. – (Syntax & semantics ; 36).

80   Okabe, Reiko: [Rev. art. of] Pylkkänen, L. (2008) *Introducing argu-
     ments. – EngL* 27/1, 2010, 172-184 | Cf. 81.

81   Pylkkänen, Liina: *Introducing arguments.* – Cambridge, MA : MIT,
     2008. – xvi, 156 p. – (Linguistic inquiry monographs ; 49).

3. Lexicon (lexicology and lexicography)

3.2. Lexicography

82   *Dictionaries : an international encyclopedia of lexicography : supple-
     mentary volume: recent developments with focus on electronic and
     computational lexicography* / Ed. by Rufus H. Gouws ; Ulrich Heid ;
     Wolfgang Schweickard ; Herbert Ernst Wiegand. – Berlin : De Gruyter
     Mouton, 2013. – xiii, 1579 p. – (Handbücher zur Sprach- und
     Kommunikationswissenschaft = Handbooks of linguistics and com-
     munication science ; 5/4).

83   Prinsloo, D. J.: The role of corpora in future dictionaries. – (38), 181-206.

3.2.2. Plurilingual lexicography

84   Beyer, Herman L.: Voorbeelde en ooradressering in tweetalige woorde-
     boeke. – *Lexikos* 21, 2011, 78-94 | E. ab: Examples and overaddressing in
     bilingual dictionaries | E. & Afrikaans ab.

85   Prinsloo, D. J.: A critical analysis of multilingual dictionaries. – *Lexikos*
     26, 2016, 220-240 | E. & Afrikaans ab.

3.5. Phraseology, paroemiology

86 *Linguo-cultural research on phraseology* / Ed.: Joanna Szerszunowicz ;
    Bogusław Nowowiejski & Priscilla Ishida ; Katsumasa Yagi. – Białystok :
    Univ. of Białystok, 2015. – 599 p. – (Intercontinental dialogue on phrase-
    ology ; 3) | E. & Pol. ab | Preface, 9-12 by Joanna Szerszunowicz.

4. Semantics and pragmatics

87 *Metaphors for learning : cross-cultural perspectives* / Ed. by Erich A.
    Berendt. – Amsterdam : Benjamins, 2008. – ix, 249 p. – (Human cogni-
    tive processing. Cognitive foundations of language structure and use ;
    22).

4.2. Pragmatics, discourse analysis and text grammar

88 *Choice in language : applications in text analysis* / Ed. by Gerard
    O'Grady ; Tom Bartlett and Lise Fontaine. – Sheffield : Equinox, 2014. –
    346 p.
89 *Contrasts and positions in information structure* / Ed. by Ivona Kučerová ;
    Ad Neeleman. – Cambridge : Cambridge UP, 2012. – vii, 346 p.

9. Psycholinguistics, language acquisition and neurolinguistics

9.3. Language acquisition

9.3.1. First language acquisition, child language

9.3.1.1. First language acquisition by pre-school children

90 *Pronouns and clitics in early language* / Ed. by María Pilar Larrañaga ;
    Pedro Guijarro-Fuentes. – Berlin : De Gruyter Mouton, 2012. – vi, 307
    p. – (Studies in generative grammar ; 108).

9.4. Neurolinguistics and language disorders

9.4.2. Language disorders

9.4.2.1. Disorders of language development

91   Southwood, Frenette; Oosthuizen, Johan: On accounting for problems demonstrated by children with SLI in the interpretation and production of passive construction. – *SPILPLUS* 36, 2008, 105-117.

10. Sociolinguistics and dialectology

10.1. Sociolinguistics

92   Boakye, Naomi: The social dimension of reading literacy development in South Africa : bridging inequalities among the various language groups. – *IJSL* 234, 2015, 133-156.

93   Dekoke, Taty: Congolese migrants and South African language appropriation. – *LM* 47/1, 2016, 84-104 | E. ab.

94   Evans, Richard: South Africa's changing linguistic frontiers : Latin mottoes in schools and universities. – *LM* 46/1, 2015, 139-156 | E. ab.

95   *Intercultural contact, language learning and migration* / Ed. by Barbara Geraghty and Jean E. Conacher. – London : Bloomsbury, 2014. – xv, 234 p. – (Advances in sociolinguistics).

96   Kaschula, Russell H.; Mostert, André; Ralarala, Monwabisi Knowledge: Communicating across cultures in South African law courts : towards an information technology solution. – *SPILPLUS* 36, 2008, 89-104.

97   Makoe, Pinky; McKinney, Carolyn: Linguistic ideologies in multilingual South African suburban schools. – *JMMD* 35/7, 2014, 658-673.

98   Mesthrie, Rajend: The risks of sociolinguistic crossing and crossovers : a retrospective from apartheid South Africa. – *SPILPLUS* 37, 2009, 89-102.

99   Mutasa, Davie E.: Language experiences of transnational migrants in the Southern African context. – *LM* 45/2, 2014, 184-203 | E. ab.

100   Nekvapil, Jiří: Sociolingvistické poznámky z Jižní Afriky. – *SaS* 73/3, 2012, 230-232 | Sociolinguistic remarks from South Africa.

101   Trimbur, John: Grassroots literacy and the written record : asbestos activism in South Africa. – *JSocL* 17/4, 2013, 460-487 | E. & Setswana ab.

102   Watermeyer, Jennifer; Penn, Claire: Communicating dosage instruc-
       tions across cultural and linguistic barriers : pharmacist-patient inter-
       actions in a South African antiretroviral clinic. – *SPILPLUS* 39, 2009,
       107-125.

103   Williams, Quentin Emmanuel; Stroud, Christopher: Multilingualism
       remixed : sampling, braggadocio and the stylisation of local voice. –
       SPIL 42, 2013, 15-36 | E. ab.

104   *Youth language practices in Africa and beyond* / Ed. by Nico
       Nassenstein ; Andrea Hollington. – Berlin : De Gruyter Mouton, 2015. –
       xi, 366 p. – (Contributions to the sociology of language ; 105).

10.1.1.   Language attitudes and social identity

105   *Bi/multilingual identity in South Africa.* – *IJBEB* – Clevedon :
       Multilingual Matters, 2014. – 635-771 – (*IJBEB* ; 17/6).

106   *The language of social media : identity and community on the internet*
       / Ed. by Philip Seargeant and Caroline Tagg. – Houndmills : Palgrave
       Macmillan, 2014. – xii, 260 p.

107   Ngwenya, Themba Lancelot: Social identity and linguistic creativity :
       manifestations of the use of multilingualism in South African adver-
       tising. – *SALALS* 29/1, 2011, 1-16.

10.1.2.   Language policy and language planning

108   Bagwasi, Mompoloki Mmangaka: Linguistic struggles within and
       beyond the Southern African Development Community. – *CILP* 13/3,
       2012, 239-248.

109   Beukes, Anne-Marie: Language policy implementation in South
       Africa : how Kempton Park's great expectations are dashed in
       Tshwane. – *SPIL* 38, 2008, 1-26.

110   Cakata, Zethu; Segalo, Puleng: Obstacles to post-apartheid language
       policy implementation : insights from language policy experts. –
       SALALS 35/4, 2017, 321-329 | E. ab.

111   Cornelius, Eleanor: Defining 'plain language' in contemporary South
       Africa. – *SPIL* 44, 2015, 1-18 | E. ab.

112   Dyers, Charlyn; Abongdia, Jane-Francis: Ideology, policy and imple-
       mentation : comparative perspectives from two African universities. –
       SPIL 43, 2014, 1-21 | On the University of Yaoundé in Cameroon and the
       University of the Western Cape in South Africa | E. ab.

113   Edwards, Viv K.; Marriote Ngwaru, Jacob: Language capital and development : the case of African language publishing for children in South Africa. – *IJSL* 225, 2014, 29-50.

114   Finlayson, Rosalie; Pienaar, Marné; Slabbert, Sarah: Metaphors of transformation : the new language of education in South Africa. – (87), 225-243.

115   Hill, Lloyd B.: Language and status : on the limits of language planning. – *SPIL* 39, 2010, 41-58 | E. ab.

116   *Language policy and the promotion of peace : African and European case studies* / Edited by Neville Alexander and Arnulf von Scheliha. – Pretoria : UNISA Press, 2014. – 154 p.

117   *Language policy in higher education : the case of medium-sized languages* / Edited by F. Xavier Vila and Vanessa Bretxa. – Bristol : Multilingual Matters, 2014. – 232 p.

118   Miti, Lazarus Musazitame: *Language rights in Southern Africa.* – Cape Town : CASAS, 2016. – 165 p. – (CASAS book series ; 118).

119   Mwaniki, Munene: *Language planning in South Africa : towards a language management approach.* – Saarbrücken : VDM Verlag Dr. Müller, 2011. – xi, 241 p.

120   Ndhlovu, Finex: The conundrums of language policy and politics in South Africa and Zimbabwe. – *AJL* 28/1, 2008, 59-80.

121   Ngcobo, Mtholeni N: The constitutional dynamism of a multilingual language policy : a case of South Africa. – *SAfrJAL* 32/2, 2012, 181-187.

122   Ngcobo, Mtholeni N: A strategic promotion of language use in multilingual South Africa : information and communication. – *SALALS* 27/1, 2009, 113-120.

123   Orman, Jon: Language and 'new' African migration to South Africa : an overview and some reflections on theoretical implications for policy and planning. – *LPol* 11/4, 2012, 301-322 | E. ab.

124   Plessis, Theo du: Die Pan-Suid-Afrikaanse Taalraad en die regulering van taalsigbaarheid in Suid-Afrika - 'n ontleding van taalregteklagtes. – *SALALS* 27/2, 2009, 173-188 | E. ab.: The Pan South African Language Board and the regulation of language visibility in South Africa - an analysis of language rights complaints | E. & Afrikaans ab., E. conclusion.

125   Plessis, Theodorus du: Language conflict and change in language visibility in South Africa's Free State Province number plate case. – *LM* 44/3, 2013, 126-148 | E. ab.

126   Prah, Kwesi Kwaa: *Nithini ngolwimi iwethu? : challenges to the promotion of indigenous languages in South Africa.* – Cape Town : CASAS, 2015. – v, 42 p. – (Monograph series [CASAS] ; 262).

127   Stroud, Christopher: The Centre for Multilingualism and Diversities
       Research at the University of the Western Cape, South Africa. –
       Multiling 1/1, 2014, 90-97.

10.2.   Multilingualism, language contact

128   *The handbook of bilingualism and multilingualism* / Ed. by Tej K.
       Bhatia ; William C. Ritchie. – Chichester : Wiley-Blackwell, 2013. – 964
       p. – (Blackwell handbooks in linguistics).

129   Loth, Chrismi-Rinda; Plessis, Theodorus du: Language visibility pat-
       terns of ergonyms in the linguistic landscape of a rural municipality
       in the southern Free State, South Africa. – *NAfr* 31/1, 2017, 11-27 | E. ab.

10.2.1.   Multilingualism

130   Hibbert, Liesel: *The linguistic landscape of post-apartheid South
       Africa : politics and discourse.* – Bristol : Multilingual Matters, 2016. –
       184 p | E. ab.

131   Makalela, Leketi: Introduction. – *IJSL* 234, 2015, 1-5 | Introd. to the
       special issue "(New) social dynamics of multilingual practices in
       the post-independent South Africa : between marginalization and
       harmonization"

132   *Multilingualism at work : from policies to practices in pub-
       lic, medical and business settings* / Ed. by Bernd Meyer ; Birgit
       Apfelbaum. – Amsterdam : Benjamins, 2010. – vi, 274 p. – (Hamburg
       studies on multilingualism ; 9).

133   Muysken, Pieter: Bridges over troubled waters : theoretical linguistics
       and multilingualism research. – *SPIL* 40, 2011, 20-38 | E. ab.

134   *(New) social dynamics of multilingual practices in the post-independent
       South Africa : between marginalization and harmonization* / Ed. by
       Leketi Makalela. – Berlin, Boston : De Gruyter, 2015 – 188 p. – (*IJSL* ;
       234) | Special issue.

135   Oostendorp, Marcelyn; Bylund, Emanuel: Emotions and HIV/AIDS in
       South Africa : a multilingual perspective. – *SPILPLUS* 41, 2012, 77-89 |
       E. ab.

136   Williams, Quentin Emmanuel; Stroud, Christopher: Multilingualism
       in transformative spaces : contact and conviviality. – *LPol* 12/4, 2013,
       289-311.

10.2.3. Language contact

137 *The Cambridge handbook of areal linguistics* / Edited by Raymond
     Hickey. – Cambridge : Cambridge UP, 2017. – xxvi, 1005 p. – (Cambridge
     handbooks in language and linguistics).
138 *Handbook of language contact* / Ed. by Raymond Hickey. –
     Chichester : Wiley-Blackwell, 2010. – xvii, 863 p. – (Blackwell hand-
     books in linguistics).
139 *Languages in contact 2011. – PhWAS* / Ed. by Zdzisław Wąsik ; Piotr P.
     Chruszczewski. – Wrocław : Wyd. Wyższej Szkoły Filologicznej we
     Wrocławiu, 2012. – 246 p. – (*PhWAS* ; 9).
140 Makalela, Leketi: Translanguaging practices in complex multilin-
     gual spaces : a discontinuous continuity in post-independent South
     Africa. – *IJSL* 234, 2015, 115-132.
141 Mesthrie, Rajend: South Africa and areal linguistics. – (137), 527-550.

11. Comparative linguistics

142 Zulu, P. N.; Botha, G.; Barnard, E.: Orthographic measures of language
     distances between the official South African languages. – *Literator*
     29/1, 2008, 185-204 | E. & Afrikaans ab.

11.1. Historical linguistics and language change

143 *Parameter theory and linguistic change* / Ed. by Charlotte Galves ; Sonia
     Cyrino ; Ruth Lopes ; Filomena Sandalo ; Juanito Avelar. – Oxford :
     Oxford UP, 2012. – xviii, 386 p. – (Oxford studies in diachronic and his-
     torical linguistics (OSDHL) ; 2).

13. Onomastics

13.2. Toponymy

144 Jenkins, Elwyn R.: Hybrid geographical names in South Africa. – *NAfr*
     31/2, 2017, 153-160 | E. ab.

13.3. Name studies other than anthroponymy and toponymy

145 [Neethling, Siebert J] Neethling, Bertie: Naming as a manifestation
     of Black Economic Empowerment (BEE) in post-1994 South Africa. –
     Onoma 43, 2008 [2010], 381-396 | E., Fr. & G. ab.

Indo-European languages

3. Indo-Iranian

3.1. Indo-Aryan (Indic)

146 *Annual review of South Asian languages and linguistics 2008* | Ed. by
Rajendra Singh. – Berlin : De Gruyter Mouton, 2008. – viii, 326 p. –
(Trends in linguistics. Studies and monographs ; 209).

147 Mesthrie, Rajend: South Africa. – (146), 237-241 | An annotated biblio.
of South African research on South Asian lgs., including Arabic and
Indian English.

3.1.3. Modern Indo-Aryan

3.1.3.5. Southern Indo-Aryan (Marathi)

148 Mesthrie, Rajend: Kokni in Cape Town [South Africa] and the socio-
linguistics of transnationalism. – *LM* 48/3, 2017, 73-97 | E. ab.

149 Mesthrie, Rajend; Kulkarni-Joshi, Sonal; Paradkar, Ruta: Documenting
125 years of Kokni in South Africa. – (12), 140-146.

9. Greek

9.3. Modern Greek

150 *Η διαχρονική συμβολή της Ελληνικής σε άλλες γλώσσες* | Επιστημονική
επιμέλεια Γεώργιος Καναράκης. – Αθήνα : Παπαζήσης, 2014. – xxvi, 746 p.

151 McDuling, Allistair; Barnes, Lawrie A.: What is the future of Greek in
South Africa? Language shift and maintenance in the Greek commu-
nity of Johannesburg. – *LM* 43/2, 2012, 166-183 | E. ab.

11.   Romance

11.3.   Gallo-Romance

11.3.2.   French

11.3.2.3.   Modern French

152   Ferreira-Meyers, Karen Aline Françoise; Horne, Fiona: Multilingualism and the language curriculum in South Africa : contextualising French within the local language ecology. – *SPILPLUS* 51, 2017, 23-40 | E. ab.

14.   Germanic

14.3.   West Germanic

14.3.1.   German

14.3.1.1.   High German

14.3.1.1.4.   New High German

153   Annas, Rolf: Fragen an die deutsche Grammatik : Schwierigkeiten von (südafrikanischen) Studenten beim Deutschlernen. – (2), 345-350 | [Questions for German grammar : difficulties of (South African) learners of German].

154   Maltzan, Carlotta von: Sprachenpolitik und die Rolle der Fremdsprachen (Deutsch) in Südafrika. – *SPILPLUS* 38, 2009, 205-214 | [Language policy and the role of foreign languages (German) in South Africa] | E. ab.

14.3.2.   Dutch

155   *Language and space : an international handbook of linguistic variation.* Vol. 3. *Dutch* / Ed. by Frans Hinskens ; Johan Taeldeman. – Berlin : De Gruyter Mouton, 2013. – xxi, 937 p., 39 maps – (Handbücher zur Sprach- und Kommunikationswissenschaft = Handbooks of linguistics and communication science ; 30/3).

14.3.2.3.   Modern Dutch

156   Flecken, Monique: Dutch in progression. – *NTaalk* 20/2, 2015, 248-252
      | Disc. of 299.

157   Fortuin, Egbert: Kirsner on imperatives and pragmatic particles. –
      NTaalk 20/2, 2015, 234-242 | Disc. of 299.

158   Geeraerts, Dirk: Dismiss polysemy? Ho maar!. – *NTaalk* 20/2, 2015, 218-
      223 | Disc. of 299.

159   Kirsner, Robert S.: Response. – *NTaalk* 20/2, 2015, 253-267 | Author's
      rejoinder to six articles discussing Robert S. Kirsner, *Qualitative-
      quantitative analyses of Dutch and Afrikaans grammar and lexicon,* cf.
      299.

160   Maes, Alfons A.: What explains demonstrative variance in Dutch? –
      NTaalk 20/2, 2015, 228-233 | Disc. of 299.

161   Steyn, J. C.: Die laaste projek van die "Hollandse taalbeweging in Suid-
      Afrika" : die Vereenvoudigde Hollandse Spelling. – *TsGw* 57/2-1, 2017,
      233-248 | The last project of the "Dutch language movement in South
      Africa" : the Simplified Dutch Spelling | E. & Afrikaans ab.

162   Weijer, Jeroen M. van de: But a short word on *maar*. – *NTaalk* 20/2,
      2015, 243-247 | Disc. of 299.

14.3.3.   Afrikaans

163   *Afrikaans : een drieluik* / Hans den Besten ; Frans L. M. P. Hinskens ; Jerzy
      Koch (red.). – Amsterdam : Stichting Neerlandistiek VU ; Münster :
      Nodus, 2009. – 255 p. – (Stichting Neerlandistiek VU ; 58).

164   Gunnink, Hilde: The grammatical structure of Sowetan tsotsitaal. –
      SALALS 32/2, 2014, 161-171.

165   *Kontemporere Afrikaanse taalkunde* / W. A. M. Carstens & N. Bosman,
      redakteurs. – Pretoria : Van Schaik, 2014. – xix, 491 p | [Contemporary
      Afrikaans linguistics].

166   Libert, Ekaterina A.: K voprosu o statuse nekotorych jazykov v zapad-
      nogermanskoj jazykovoj podgruppe (afrikaans, idiš, plotdič). – *SFŽ* 3,
      2010, 186-190 | On the status of some languages of the West-Germanic
      group (Afrikaans, Yiddish, Low German).

167   Noordegraaf, Jan: Koloniaal Nederlands in verandering Afrikaans
      versus Amerikaans Leeg Duits. – *AUW* 3619, *NeerlW* 24, 2014, 67-91 |
      Colonial Dutch in motion: South African Dutch versus American Low
      Dutch | E. ab.

168   Rooy, Bertus van: Die Afrikaanse taalkunde van toeka tot nou. – (165),
      1-26 | [Afrikaans linguistics from past to present].

169   *Taalportaal : the linguistics of Dutch, Frisian and Afrikaans online* |
      Online resource | Presentation by the authors, cf. 170.

170   [Wouden, Anton van der] Wouden, Ton van der; Audring, Jenny;
      Bennis, Hans; Beukema, Frits; Booij, Geert E.; Broekhuis, Hans; Corver,
      Norbert; Cremers, Crit; Dernison, Roderik; Dikken, Marcel den; Dyk,
      Siebren; Gussenhoven, Carlos [Haan, Germen J de] Haan, Ger de;
      Heuven, Vincent J. van; Hoekstra, Eric; Hoekstra, Jarich; Hoogeveen,
      Bart; Jong, Gerbrich de; [Keizer, M Evelien] Keizer, Evelien; Kirstein,
      Anna; Köhnlein, Björn; Landsbergen, Frank; Linke, Kathrin;
      Oostendorp, Marc van; Ouddeken, Nina; Sebregts, Koen; Tiberius,
      Carole; Versloot, Arjen P.; Visser, Willem; Vos, Riet; Vries, Truus de;
      Weening, Joke: Het Taalportaal : een nieuwe wetenschappelijke gram-
      matica voor het Nederlands en het Fries (en het Afrikaans). – *NTaalk*
      21/1, 2016, 157-168 | Taalportaal : a new scientific grammar of Dutch
      and Frisian (and Afrikaans) | E. ab | Cf. 169.

0.2.4.   ORGANIZATIONS

171   Odendaal, Gerda: Die rol van die US se Departement Afrikaans en
      Nederlands in die ontwikkeling van die Afrikaanse leksikografie :
      die Nederlands-Afrikaans-stryd gedurende die aanvangsjare. – *TsGw*
      56/1, 2016, 257-276 | The role of Stellenbosch University's Department
      of Afrikaans and Dutch in the development of Afrikaans lexicogra-
      phy : the Dutch-Afrikaans battle during the formative years | E. &
      Afrikaans ab.

0.3.   LINGUISTIC THEORY AND METHODOLOGY

172   Breed, Adri; Carstens, Wannie A. M.; Olivier, Jako: Die DBAT : 'n
      onbekende digitale taalkundemuseum. – *TsGw* 56/2-1, 2016, 391-409
      | The DBAL : an unknown digital language museum | *DBAT = Digitale
      Bibliografie van die Afrikaanse Taalkunde* ("Digital Bibliography of
      Afrikaans Linguistics") | E. & Afrikaans ab.

173   Huyssteen, Gerhard B. van; Botha, Melodi; Antonites, Alex: Die
      Virtuele Instituut vir Afrikaans (VivA) en markbehoeftes in die
      Afrikaanse gemeenskap. – *TsGw* 56/2-1, 2016, 410-437 | The Virtual
      Institute for Afrikaans and the Afrikaans community's market needs |
      E. & Afrikaans ab.

0.6. APPLIED LINGUISTICS

174 [Fourie, Hanelle] Fourie Blair, Hanelle: Ekwivalentverhoudings in tweetalige woordeboeke : implikasies vir die databasis van 'n elektroniese tweetalige woordeboek van Suid-Afrikaanse Gebaretaal en Afrikaans. – *Lexikos* 25, 2015, 151-169 | Equivalent relations in bilingual dictionaries : implications for the database of an electronic bilingual dictionary of South African Sign Language AND Afrikaans | E. & Afrikaans ab.

175 Oort, Ronel van; Carstens, Wannie A. M.: Die onderrig van Afrikaanse woordeskat en variëteite vanuit 'n inklusiewe taalgeskiedkundige perspektief = Teaching Afrikaans vocabulary and varieties from an inclusive language-historical perspective. – *TsGw* 54/4, 2014, 693-707 | E. & Afrikaans ab.

1.1. PHONETICS

176 Wissing, Daan P.: Fonetiek. – (165), 91-125 | [Phonetics].

1.1.2. ACOUSTIC PHONETICS

177 Coetzee, Andries W.; Beddor, Patricia Speeter; Bouavichith, Dominique; Craft, Justin T.: Fo and plosive voicing in Afrikaans. – *JASA* 140/1, 2016, 3106 | E. ab.

178 Wissing, Daan P.: Ontronding in Afrikaans. – *TsGw* 51/1, 2011, 1-20 | E. ab.: Derounding in Afrikaans.

179 Wissing, Daan P.: Oor die status van die "oe" in Afrikaans : 'n akoestiese analise. – *TsGw* 50/1, 2010, 31-49 | E. ab.: On the status of "oe" in Afrikaans : an acoustic analysis | On the Afrikaans vowel /u/

180 Wissing, Daan P.; Pienaar, Wikus; Niekerk, Daniel van: Palatalisation of /s/ in Afrikaans. – *SPILPLUS* 48, 2015, 137-158 | E. ab.

1.2. PHONOLOGY

181 Bennett, William G.: Agreement, dependencies, and Surface Correspondence in Obolo and beyond. – *SPILPLUS* 44, 2014, 149-171 | E. ab | Commentary cf. 183 | Author's rejoinder cf. 645.

182 Besten, Hans den: In search of a submerged phonology : the case of early Cape Dutch Pidgin. – (37), 219-241.

1.3.   MOR(PHO)PHONOLOGY

2.   GRAMMAR, MORPHOSYNTAX

195   Ellis, Carla; Conradie, Simone; Huddlestone, Kate: The acquisition of grammatical gender in L2 German by learners with Afrikaans, English or Italian as their L1. – *SPIL* 41, 2012, 17-27 | E. ab.

196   Rosenbach, Anette: Constraints in contact : animacy in English and Afrikaans genitive variation – a cross-linguistic perspective. – *Glossa* 2/1, 2017, 72 | E. ab.

2.1.   MORPHOLOGY AND WORD-FORMATION

197   Butler, Anneke: Die deelwoord as 'n ánder vorm van die werkwoord. – *TsGw* 56/1, 2016, 81-101 | The participle as a different form of the verb | E. & Afrikaans ab.

198   Huyssteen, Gerhard B. van: Morfologie. – (165), 171-208 | [Morphology].

199   Kürschner, Sebastian: Morphological non-blocking in Dutch plural allomorphy : a contrastive approach. – *STUF* 62/4, 2009, 285-306.

200   Prędota, Stanisław: Morfologia języka niderlandzkiego i języka afrikaans. – (15), 387-399 | Dutch and Afrikaans morphology | G. ab.

201   Prędota, Stanisław: On the morphology of Dutch and Afrikaans. – *PhWAS* 4, 2011, 143-152.

2.1.2.   DERIVATIONAL MORPHOLOGY

202   Besten, Hans den: Reduplication in Afrikaans / With Carla Luijks and Paul T. Roberge. – (509), 195-219 | First publ. in 1043.

2.2.   SYNTAX

203   Berghoff, Robyn: Movement in the Afrikaans left periphery : a view from anti-locality. – *SPIL* 48, 2017, 35-50 | E. ab.

204   Besten, Hans den: Afrikaans relative 'wat' and West-Germanic relativization systems. – (509), 41-59 | Translation of 190.

205   Besten, Hans den: The complex ancestry of the Afrikaans associative constructions. – (509), 25-33 | First publ. in 2001.

206   Besten, Hans den: Double negation and the genesis of Afrikaans. – (509), 221-256 | First publ. in 1987.

207   Besten, Hans den: Is there "preposition stranding in COMP" in Afrikaans? No way!. – (45), 57-63.

208   Besten, Hans den: The origins of the Afrikaans pre-nominal possessive system(s). – (509), 7-23.

209   Besten, Hans den: What a little word can do for you : *wat* in Afrikaans possessive relatives. – (509), 35-39 | First publ. in 1999 | Appendix to LB 1983, 8577 and 190.

210   Biberauer, Theresa: Doubling vs. omission : insights from Afrikaans negation. – (79), 103-140.

211   Biberauer, Theresa; Potgieter, Jean-Marie: Negative exclamatives in Afrikaans : some initial thoughts. – *SPIL* 48, 2017, 17-33 | E. ab.

212   Biberauer, Theresa; Zeijlstra, Hedde: Negative changes : three factors and the diachrony of Afrikaans negation. – (143), 238-264.

213   Botha, Morné; Oosthuizen, Johan: Die struktuur van die linker-sins-grens in Afrikaans. – *SPILPLUS* 37, 2009, 1-68 | [The structure of the left sentence boundary in Afrikaans].

214   Breed, Adri; Brisard, Frank: Postulêre werkwoorde as progressiewe merkers in Afrikaans en Nederlands. – *IN* 53/1, 2015, 3-28 | E. ab.

215   Breed, Adri; Brisard, Frank; Verhoeven, Ben: Periphrastic progressive constructions in Dutch and Afrikaans : a contrastive analysis. – *JGL-SGL* 29/4, 2017, 305-378 | E. ab.

216   Colleman, Timothy; Feinauer, Ilse; Braeckeveldt, Charlotte: Over lexicale voorkeuren in de alternantie tussen de "skoon bysin" en de "*dat*-bysin" : een distinctieve collexeemanalyse. – *TsGw* 56/1, 2016, 117-133 | On lexical preferences in the alternation between the *skoon bysin* "bare complement clause" and the *dat-bysin* "*that*-complement clause" : a distinctive collexeme analysis | E. & Afrikaans ab.

217   Conradie, C. Jac: Willens en wetens : perspektiewe op die Afrikaanse werkwoord *wil*. – *TsGw* 56/1, 2016, 7-24 | Willing and knowing : perspectives on the Afrikaans verb *wil* | E. & Afrikaans ab.

218   Corver, Norbert; Koppen, Marjo van: NP-ellipsis with adjectival remnants : a micro-comparative perspective. – *NLLT* 29/2, 2011, 371-421 | A contrastive analysis of Afrikaans, (standard & dialectal) Dutch, Frisian and English.

219   Feinauer, Ilse; Ponelis, Fritz: Basiese Afrikaanse sintaksis. – (165), 209-242 | [Basic Afrikaans syntax].

220   [Horst, Johannes M van der] Horst, Joop van der: Vaste werkwoordeli-jke verbindingen in het Nederlands en het Afrikaans. – *TNA* 15/1, 2008, 29-43 | [Fixed verbal combinations in Dutch and Afrikaans] | E. ab.

221   Huddlestone, Kate: *Negative indefinites in Afrikaans*. – Utrecht : LOT, 2010. – xvi, 331 p. – (LOT dissertation series ; 250) | Utrecht Univ. diss.

222   Huddlestone, Kate; Swart, Henriëtte de: A bidirectional Optimality Theoretic analysis of multiple negative indefinites in Afrikaans. – *SPIL* 43, 2014, 137-164 | E. ab.

223   Jordaan, Adéle: Afrikaanse verbandsmerkers : uitbreiding en her-
       kategorisering van voorbeeldwoorde. – *SALALS* 34/2, 2016, 147-167 |
       Afrikaans transition markers : expansion and reclassification of exam-
       ple words | Afrikaans ab.

224   Kampen, Jacqueline van: Afrikaans directionality switch in 'triple'
       V-clusters with the auxiliary *het*. – *LIN* 34, 2017, 77-91 | E. ab.

225   Kirsten, Johanita: The use of was in Afrikaans passive constructions :
       a diachronic corpus study. – *SALALS* 33/2, 2015, 159-170.

226   Kirsten, Johanita: Veranderinge in adverbiale tydsverwysing in
       Afrikaans van 1911 tot 2010. – *TsGw* 56/1, 2016, 45-61 | Changes in adver-
       bial temporal reference in Afrikaans from 1911 to 2010 | E. & Afrikaans
       ab.

227   Kotzé, Ernst F.: Aspects of congruence and divergence relating to
       adjectives in Dutch and Afrikaans. – *NTaalk* 21/2, 2016, 215-227 | E. ab.

228   Messerschmidt, J. J. E.: Die gebruik van die onderskikker *wanneer* in
       hipotaktiese verbindings. – *TsGw* 49/1, 2009, 160-178 | E. ab.: The use of
       the subordinating conjunction "wanneer" (when) in hypotactic bind-
       ing | E. & Afrikaans ab.

229   Messerschmidt, J. J. E.: Die gebruik van die voegwoord *wanneer*
       in bysinsinlywing. – *TsGw* 48/1, 2008, 23-40 | E. ab.: The use of the
       Afrikaans conjunction "wanneer" (when) in subordinate clause
       embedding.

230   Messerschmidt, J. J. E.; Messerschmidt, H. J.: Voorwaardelike kon-
       struksies met *indien* soos gebruik in wetenskaplike tydskrifte (deel 2:
       gemerkte konstruksies). – *TsGw* 52/2, 2012, 271-289 | E. ab.: Conditional
       constructions using "indien" in scientific journals (part 2: marked con-
       structions) | Cf. 312.

231   Oosthuizen, Johan: Obligatory reflexivity in a Minimalist grammar of
       Afrikaans. – *SPILPLUS* 42, 2013, 205-241 | E. ab.

232   Oosthuizen, Johan: *Obligatory reflexivity in Afrikaans : a minimalist
       approach.* – Stellenbosch : Universiteit van Stellenbosch, 2013. – [7],
       186 p. | Diss. at Univ. of Stellenbosch, March 2013 | E. & Afrikaans ab.

233   Oosthuizen, Johan: Reflexives and reflexive constructions in
       Afrikaans. – *SPILPLUS* 47, 2015, 99-127 | E. ab.

234   Potgieter, Anneke Perold: A comparative analysis of passive construc-
       tions in English, Afrikaans and isiXhosa : grammar and acquisition. –
       SPIL 47, 2017, 27-66 | E. ab.

235   Pretorius, Erin: Having fun with *van* : a Nanosyntactic take on syncre-
       tism. – *SPILPLUS* 42, 2013, 243-261 | E. ab.

236 Pretorius, Erin; Oosthuizen, Johan: A nanosyntactic analysis of Afrikaans passive participles. – *SALALS* 30/4, 2012, 449-467.

237 Pretorius, Erin: The secret nominal life of Afrikaans intransitive adpositions. – *SPIL* 48, 2017, 9-16 | E. ab.

238 Pretorius, Erin: *Spelling out P : a unified syntax of Afrikaans adpositions and V-particles.* – Utrecht : LOT, 2017. – xiv, 349 p. – (LOT dissertation series ; 363) | Diss. at the Univ. of Utrecht, 2 June 2017 | Du. summary p. 341-345.

239 Rooy, Bertus van; Kruger, Haidee: Faktore wat die weglating van die Afrikaanse onderskikker *dat* bepaal. – *TsGw* 56/1, 2016, 102-116 | Factors that determine the omission of the Afrikaans complementiser *dat* "that" | E. & Afrikaans ab.

240 Taraldsen, Knut Tarald: NPE, gender and the countable/mass distinction. – *SPIL* 48, 2017, 161-181 | E. ab | NPE = noun phrase ellipsis.

241 Vos, Mark de: Afrikaans mixed adposition orders as a PF-linearization effect. – (34), 333-357.

242 Wet, Annette de; Ferreira,Camille: Sintaktiese patroonmatighede in advertensietaal. – *SALALS* 35/1, 2017, 121-134 | [Syntactic patterns in advertising language] | E. & Afrikaans ab.

243 [Zwart, C. Jan Wouter] Zwart, Jan-Wouter: A note on the periphrastic past in Afrikaans. – *SPIL* 48, 2017, 1-8 | E. ab.

3.2. LEXICOGRAPHY

244 Gouws, Rufus H.: Aspects of Afrikaans lexicography. – (82), 827-835.

245 Gouws, Rufus H.: Enkele minder bekende Afrikaanse woordeboekmonumente. – *TsGw* 56/2-1, 2016, 355-370 | A few lesser known Afrikaans dictionary monuments | E. & Afrikaans ab.

246 Gouws, Rufus H.: Leksikografie. – (165), 373-407 | [Lexicography].

247 Gouws, Rufus H.: Die leksikografiese aanbieding en behandeling van vaste uitdrukkings. – *Lexikos* 23, 2013, 135-149 | E. ab.: The lexicographic presentation and treatment of fixed expressions | E. & Afrikaans ab.

248 Merwe, Michele F. van der: Kriteria vir woordeboekwerkboeke in Afrikaans. – (43), 280-294 | Criteria for dictionary workbooks in Afrikaans | E. & Fr. ab.

249 Odendaal, Gerda: Die rol van die US se Departement Afrikaans en Nederlands in die ontwikkeling van die Afrikaanse leksikografie onder Nederlandse invloed : verklarende standaardwoordeboeke. – *Lexikos* 26, 2016, 193-219 | The role of Stellenbosch University's department of Afrikaans and Dutch in the development of Afrikaans lexicography : development under Dutch influence | E. & Afrikaans ab.

250 Plessis, André du: A functional analysis of the e-WAT with specific focus on the mobile version : towards a model for improvement. – *Lexikos* 24, 2014, 75-93 | E. & Afrikaans ab.

251 Plessis, André du: Die rol van die bruikbaarheidsbenadering binne die e-leksikografie. – *Literator* 38/2, 2017, 11 p. | The role of usability in e-lexicography | E. & Afrikaans ab.

252 Prinsloo, D. J.: The quality, relevance and usefulness of ever-increasing amounts of internet data to lexicography : the case of Afrikaans. – *Lexicographica* 28, 2012, 3-11.

253 Prinsloo, D. J.; Taljard, Elsabé: Afrikataalleksikografie : gister, vandag en môre. – *Lexikos* 27, 2017, 427-456 | African language lexicography : yesterday, today and tomorrow | E. & Afrikaans ab.

254 Prinsloo, D. J.: Die verifiëring, verfyning en toepassing van leksiko-grafiese liniale vir Afrikaans. – *Lexikos* 20, 2010, 390-409 | E. ab.: The verification, refinement and application of lexicographic rulers for Afrikaans | E. & Afrikaans ab.

255 Smit, Maria: Rufus Gouws se rol in die bekendstelling van H. E. Wiegand se metaleksikografie en terminologie in die Suider-Afrikaanse konteks. – (43), 244-258 | Rufus Gouws's role in the introduction of H. E. Wiegand's metalexicography and terminology in the Southern African context | E. & Afrikaans ab.

256 Tarp, Sven; Gouws, Rufus H.: Skoolwoordeboeke vir huistaalleerders van Afrikaans. – *Lexikos* 20, 2010, 466-494 | E. ab.: School dictionaries for home language learners of Afrikaans | E. & Afrikaans ab.

3.2.1. MONOLINGUAL LEXICOGRAPHY

257 *Afrikaanse woordelys en spelreëls* | saamgestel deur die Taalkommissie van die Suid-Afrikaanse Akademie vir Wetenskap en Kuns. – Kaapstad : Pharos, 2017. – xxxiii, 757 p. | [Afrikaans word list and spelling rules].

258 Ball, Liezl H.; Bothma, Theo J. D.: A usability evaluation of the proto-type *Afrikaanse idiome-woordeboek*. – *Lexikos* 27, 2017, 78-106 | E. & Afrikaans ab.

259 [Bosman, Nerina] Bosman, N.; Otto, Anna Nel: Die hantering van new-eskikkers en onderskikkers in Afrikaanse woordeboeke. – *Lexikos* 22, 2012, 69-85 | E. ab.: The treatment of coordinating and subordinating conjunctions in Afrikaans dictionaries | E. & Afrikaans ab.

260   Bosman, Nerina; Taljard, Elsabé; [Prinsloo, D. J.] Prinsloo, Danie:
       Honderd jaar *Afrikaanse Woordelys en Spelreëls* : 'n oorsig en waarder-
       ing. Deel 1: Die woordelys. – *TsGw* 57/2-1, 2017, 285-301 | One hundred
       years of *Afrikaanse Woordelys en Spelreëls* : an overview and evalua-
       tion. Part 1: The wordlist | E. & Afrikaans ab.

261   Botha, Willem F.: Ensiklopedisiteit in die *Woordeboek van die
       Afrikaanse taal* : 'n "saak" van balans. – *Lexikos* 19, 2009, 23-33 | E. ab.

262   *Elektroniese WAT (Woordeboek van die Afrikaanse taal, A tot R)*. –
       Stellenbosch : Buro van die WAT, 2009. – CD-Rom.

263   Feinauer, A. E.: Die agste deel van die *Woordeboek van die Afrikaanse
       Taal*. – *TsGw* 33/4, 1993, 286-298 | Rev. art. on 73 | E. ab.

264   Feinauer, Ilse: Doen die *Woordeboek van die Afrikaanse taal deel XII* dit
       vir die Afrikaanse taal en die Suid-Afrikaanse leksikografie? – *Lexikos*
       17, 2007, 259-277 | E. & Afrikaans ab | Rev. art. of 276.

265   Feinauer, Ilse: Die negende deel van die *Woordeboek van die Afrikaanse
       Taal*. – *Lexikos* 6, 1996, 233-271 | E. & Afrikaans ab | Rev. art. on 274, 9.

266   Huyssteen, Gerhard B. van: Die aard, doel en omvang van die
       Afrikaanse Woordelys en Spelreëls. Deel 1. – *TsGw* 57/2-1, 2017, 323-345
       | The nature, goal, and scope of the *Afrikaanse Woordelys en Spelreëls*.
       Part 1 | E. & Afrikaans ab.

267   Huyssteen, Gerhard B. van: Opname- en elimineringskriteria vir die
       Afrikaanse Woordelys en Spelreëls : die geval *emeritus*. Deel 2. – *TsGw*
       57/2-1, 2017, 346-368 | Inclusion and elimination criteria for the
       Afrikaanse Woordelys en Spelreëls : the case of *emeritus*. Part 2 | E. &
       Afrikaans ab.

268   Labuschagne, F. J.; Eksteen, L. C.: *Verklarende Afrikaanse woorde-
       boek*. – Kaapstad : Pharos, 2010. – xiv, 1580 p | 8th ed. cf. 269.

269   Labuschagne, F. J.; Eksteen, L. C.: *Verklarende Afrikaanse woorde-
       boek*. – Pretoria : Van Schaik, 1993. – 1117 p.

270   Otto, Anna Nel: 'n Kritiese waardering van die *Afrikaanse Woordelys
       en Spelreëls – AWS* (2009). – *TsGw* 57/2-1, 2017, 271-284 | A critical
       appraisal of the *Afrikaanse Woordelys en Spelreëls – AWS* (2009) | E. &
       Afrikaans ab.

271   Otto, Anna Nel: 'n Kritiese waardering van die hantering van kolloka-
       sies en idiome in die HAT (2005). – (43), 188-195 | A critical apprecia-
       tion of the treatment of collocations and idioms in the *HAT* (2005)
       | *HAT = Verklarende Handwoordeboek van die Afrikaanse Taal* | E. &
       Afrikaans ab.

272 Swanepoel, Piet H.: Evalueringskriteria en die interaksie tussen die leksikografieteorie en -praktyk : die ontwerp van die *Woordeboek van die Afrikaanse taal* as gevallestudie. – *Lexikos* 24, 2014, 378-401 | E. ab.: Evaluation criteria and the interaction between lexicographic theory and practice : the design of the *Woordeboek van die Afrikaanse taal* as case study | E. & Afrikaans ab | Cf. 278.

273 Taljard, Elsabé; [Prinsloo, D. J.] Prinsloo, Danie; Bosman, Nerina: Honderd jaar *Afrikaanse Woordelys en Spelreëls* : 'n oorsig en waardering. Deel 2: Die gebruiker in fokus. – *TsGw* 57/2-1, 2017, 302-322 | One hundred years of *Afrikaanse Woordelys en Spelreëls* : an overview and evaluation. Part 2: The user in focus | E. & Afrikaans ab.

274 *Woordeboek van die Afrikaanse taal.* Tiende deel. *M* / Hoofdred. D. J. van Schalkwyk ; eindred. J. C. M. D. du Plessis ; bestuurder red. steundienste Pieter Harteveld ; senior medered. F. J. Lombard ; medered. Marié M. Nel ; Willem F. Botha ; Aletta E. van Niekerk ; medered. (termyn) Liza Rademeyer ; G. J. van Wyk ; B. P. D. Gabriels. – Stellenbosch : Buro van die WAT, 1996. – xx, 660 p | Cf. 280 & 265.

275 *Woordeboek van die Afrikaanse taal.* Elfde deel. *N - O* / Hoofdred. D. J. van Schalkwyk ; eindred. J. C. M. D. du Plessis ; senior medered. F. J. Lombard ; medered. Willem F. Botha ; G. J. van Wyk ; medered. (termyn) Liza Rademeyer ; B. P. D. Gabriels ; P. A. Louw. – Stellenbosch : Buro van die WAT, 2000. – xxii, 935 p | Cf. 274.

276 *Woordeboek van die Afrikaanse taal.* Twaalfde deel. *P-Q* / Hoofredakteur Willem F. Botha ; eindredakteur F. J. Lombard ; senior mederedakteur G. J. van Wyk ; mederedakteurs Liza Rademeyer ; B. P. D. Gabriels ; Phillip A. Louw. – Stellenbosch : Buro van die WAT, 2005. – xxiii, 760 p. | Cf. 275.

277 *Woordeboek van die Afrikaanse taal.* Dertiende deel. *R* / Hoofredakteur Willem F. Botha ; eindredakteur F. J. Lombard ; senior mederedakteur G. J. van Wyk ; mederedakteurs Liza Rademeyer ; B. P. D. Gabriels ; Aletta E. Cloete ; Hanelle Fourie. – Stellenbosch : Buro van die WAT, 2009. – xxi, 541 p. | Cf. 276.

278 *Woordeboek van die Afrikaanse taal.* XIV. *S - Skooi* / Hoofred.: W. F. Botha. – Stellenbosch : Buro van die WAT, 2013. – xxi, 674 p. | Cf. 277.

279 *Woordeboek van die Afrikaanse taal.* Agste deel. *kos - kyw-* / Hoofdred. D. C. Hauptfleisch ; assistent-hoofred. J. C. M. D. du Plessis; senior medered. D. J. van Schalkwyk ; medered. Pieter Harteveld [et al.]. – Stellenbosch : Buro van die WAT, 1991. – xxiii, 584 p.

280   *Woordeboek van die Afrikaanse taal.* Negende deel. *L* / Hoofdred. D. J.
      van Schalkwyk ; eindred. J. C. M. D. du Plessis ; bestuurder red. steun-
      dienste Pieter Harteveld ; senior medered. F. J. Lombard ; medered.
      Marié M. Nel ; Willem F. Botha ; Aletta E. van Niekerk. – Stellenbosch :
      Buro van die WAT, 1994. – xxii, 516 p. | Cf. 279.

3.2.2.   PLURILINGUAL LEXICOGRAPHY

281   Bergenholtz, Henning; Bothma, Theo J. D.; Gouws, Rufus H.: A
      model for integrated dictionaries of fixed expressions. – (10), 34-42 |
      Electronic publ.

282   Beyer, Herman L.: Die naslaanpotensiaal van lemmakandidate vir 'n
      monofunksionele beknopte Nederlands-Afrikaans-woordeboek. –
      SPILPLUS 47, 2015, 19-33 | The consultation potential of lemma candi-
      dates for a monofunctional concise Dutch-Afrikaans dictionary | E. &
      Afrikaans ab.

283   Conradie, C. Jac: Het "Beknopt Afrikaans-Nederlands woordenboek
      met Engelse equivalenten" van A. A. F. Teurlinckx. – *AUW* 3472,
      NeerlW 21, 2012, 127-139 | E. ab.

284   Fourie, Hanelle: *'n Leksikografiese model vir 'n elektroniese tweet-
      alige grondslagfasewoordeboek van Suid-Afrikaanse Gebaretaal en
      Afrikaans.* – Stellenbosch : Universiteit van Stellenbosch, 2013. – [16],
      446 p. | [Lexicographical model for an electronic bilingual diction-
      ary of South African Sign Language and Afrikaans] | Diss. at Univ. of
      Stellenbosch, March 2013 | E. & Afrikaans ab.

285   Gouws, Rufus H.: *ANNA* : 'n nuwe leksikografiese benadering met
      nuwe strukture vir ou funksies en gevestigde gebruikers. – *TNA* 18/2,
      2011, 3-13 | *ANNA* : a new lexicographic approach with new structures
      for old functions and established users | E. ab.

286   Gouws, Rufus H.; Leroyer, Patrick: Verhoogde leksikografiese toegank-
      likheid in die oorgang van 'n toeristewoordeboek na 'n toeristegids
      as naslaanbron. – *TsGw* 49/1, 2009, 145-159 | E. ab.: Increased lexico-
      graphic accessibility in the transition from a tourist dictionary to a
      tourist guide | E. & Afrikaans ab.

287   Gouws, Rufus H.; Prinsloo, D. J.: Surrogaatekwivalensie in tweetalige
      woordeboeke met spesifieke verwysing na zero-ekwivalensie in
      Afrikataalwoordeboeke. – *TsGw* 50/4, 2010, 502-519 | E. ab.: Surrogate
      equivalence in bilingual dictionaries with specific reference to zero
      equivalence in dictionaries for African languages | E. & Afrikaans ab.

288 Kotzé, Ernst F.: 'n Ortografiese brug tussen Japannees en Afrikaans :
     die keuse van 'n romeinse transliterasiesisteem. – *TsGw* 56/2-1, 2016,
     438-453 | An orthographic bridge between Japanese and Afrikaans :
     the choice of a roman transliteration system | E. & Afrikaans ab.

289 Martin, Willy: Amalgamated bilingual dictionaries. – (44), 437-449.

290 Martin, Willy: *ANNA* : een WOORDENBOEK met een NAAM (en wat
     er ACHTER steekt). – *TNA* 18/2, 2011, 14-27 | [*ANNA* : a dictionary with
     a name (and what lies behind it)] | E. ab.

291 Potgieter, Liezl: Leksikografiese seleksie as deel van die samestel-
     lingsproses van 'n vakwoordeboek vir vertalers. – (43), 196-211 |
     Lexicographic selection as part of the compilation process of a spe-
     cialist dictionary for translators | E. & Afrikaans ab.

292 Prinsloo, D. J.: 'n Kritiese beskouing van woordeboeke met geamalga-
     meerde lemmalyste. – *Lexikos* 23, 2013, 371-393 | E. ab.: A critical exam-
     ination of dictionaries with amalgamated lemmalists | E. & Afrikaans
     ab.

3.3. ETYMOLOGY

293 Bergerson, Jeremy: On the origin of the Afrikaans pronoun *watter*. –
     NOWELE 60 61, 2011, 171-185.

294 Prinsloo, Anton F.: *Die aap in jou koffie : Afrikaanse eponieme van A tot
     Z.* – Pretoria : Protea Boekhuis, 2011. – 351 p | [The monkey in your cof-
     fee : Afrikaans eponyms from A to Z].

3.4. TERMINOLOGY

295 Beukes, Anne-Marie; Pienaar, Marné: Die vertaling van 'n vertaalter-
     minologielys in Afrikaans : 'n prosesbeskryving. – (41), 61-74 | [The
     translation of translating terminology in Afrikaans : a description of
     the process] | Afrikaans ab.

296 Cornelius, Eleanor; Pienaar, Marné: Die vertaling en lokalisering van
     terminologie van het tolken vir 'n Suid-Afrikaanse teikengehoor. –
     SPIL 47, 2017, 181-201 | [The translation and localization of interpreter
     terminology for a South African target audience] | E. ab.

3.5. PHRASEOLOGY, PAROEMIOLOGY

297 Prędota, Stanisław: On the morphology of proverbs in Afrikaans and
     Dutch. – *AJMPh* 1, 2012, 99-106.

4.   SEMANTICS AND PRAGMATICS

298   Boogaart, Ronny; Foolen, Ad: Discussion of Robert S. Kirsner, *Qualitative-quantitative analyses of Dutch and Afrikaans grammar and lexicon.* – *NTaalk* 20/2, 2015, 215-217 | Introd. to six articles discussing 299.

299   Kirsner, Robert S.: *Qualitative-quantitative analyses of Dutch and Afrikaans grammar and lexicon.* – Amsterdam : Benjamins, 2014. – xi, 239 p. – (Studies in functional and structural linguistics ; 67) | Disc. cf. 298 ; 158 ; 59 ; 160 ; 157 ; 162 ; 156 ; and author's rejoinder, cf. 159.

4.1.   SEMANTICS

300   Bosman, Nerina; Pienaar, Marné: Afrikaanse semantiek. – (165), 245-274 | [Afrikaans semantics].

301   Bylund, Emanuel; Athanasopoulos, Panos; Oostendorp, Marcelyn: Motion event cognition and grammatical aspect : evidence from Afrikaans. – *Linguistics* 51/5, 2013, 929-955.

302   Niekerk, Angelique van; Lubbe, Elmarie: Retoriese stylfigure as intellektuele spel in advertensiekommunikasie = Rhetorical figures as intellectual play in advertising communication. – *TsGw* 54/3, 2014, 446-462 | E. & Afrikaans ab.

4.1.1.   LEXICAL SEMANTICS

303   [Bosman, Nerina] Bosman, N.: EET en DRINK in Afrikaans : 'n leksikaal-semantiese ondersoek = EATING and DRINKING in Afrikaans : a lexical semantic study. – *TsGw* 55/1, 2015, 123-146 | E. & Afrikaans ab.

304   Carney, Terrence R.: 'n Forensies-semantiese beskouing van die woordgebruik 'onkoste' in die hofsaak *Commissioner for South African Revenue Service vs. Labat Africa Limited.* – *SALALS* 30/4, 2012, 487-496.

4.1.2.   GRAMMATICAL SEMANTICS

305   Biberauer, Theresa; Zeijlstra, Hedde: Negative concord in Afrikaans : filling a typological gap. – *JSem* 29/3, 2012, 345-371.

306   Breed, Adri: The subjective use of postural verb in Afrikaans (I) : evolution from progressive to modal. – *SPILPLUS* 52, 2017, 1-21 | E. ab.

307   Breed, Adri: The subjective use of postural verbs in Afrikaans (II) : a
      corpus analysis of *CPV en* in Zefrikaans. – *SPILPLUS* 52, 2017, 23-43 |
      E. ab.

308   Conradie, C. Jac: Is *regtig* rêrig Duits *richtig*? – *TsGw* 51/4, 2011, 716-729
      | Is *regtig* really German *richtig*?

309   Fouché, Nadine; Berg, Ria van den; Olivier, Jako: Carstens se raamwerk
      van Afrikaanse konjunksiemerkers : 'n akkurater en vollediger weer-
      gawe. – *TsGw* 57/3, 2017, 814-836 | Carstens's framework of Afrikaans
      conjunction markers : a more accurate and complete version | E. &
      Afrikaans ab.

310   Kirsner, Robert S.: Instructional meanings, iconicity, and *l'arbitraire
      du signe* in the analysis of the Afrikaans demonstratives. – (64), 97-137.

311   Messerschmidt, J. J. E.; Bergh, Luna: Met kerse op *met*-konstruks-
      ies : 'n verwysingspuntperspektief. – *SALALS* 29/1, 2011, 97-113 | E. &
      Afrikaans ab.

312   Messerschmidt, J. J. E.; Messerschmidt, H. J.: Voorwaardelike kon-
      struksies met *indien* soos gebruik in wetenskaplike tydskrifte (deel 1 :
      basiese konstruksies). – *TsGw* 51/2, 2011, 124-141 | E. ab.: Conditional
      constructions with "indien" (if), as used in scientific journals (part 1 :
      basic constructions).

4.2.   PRAGMATICS, DISCOURSE ANALYSIS AND TEXT GRAMMAR

313   Anthonissen, Christine; Meyer, Bernd: Question-answer sequences
      between doctors and patients in a South African HIV/AIDS day
      clinic. – *SPILPLUS* 36, 2008, 1-34.

314   Conradie, C. Jac: Die gebruik van Afrikaanse modale partikels deur
      voormalige Khoisprekers. – *SPILPLUS* 47, 2015, 35-57 | The use of
      Afrikaans modal particles by former Khoi speakers | E. & Afrikaans ab.

315   Conradie, C. Jac: What is inherent in a word? : a look at Dutch *eigen-
      lijk*, Afrikaans *eintlik* and German *eigentlich*. – *GermL* 206-209, 2010,
      365-394.

316   Jantjies, Wesley; Dulm, Ondene van: *Mos* as a discourse marker in
      rural Cape Afrikaans. – *LM* 43/1, 2012, 3-20 | E. ab.

317   Niekerk, Angelique van: A discourse-analytical approach to intertex-
      tual advertisements : a model to describe a dominant world-view. –
      SALALS 26/4, 2008, 495-512.

318   Niekerk, Angelique van; Olivier, Jako: Pragmatiek. – (165), 275-309 |
      [Pragmatics].

319   Simon, Horst J.: Zur Grammatik der indirekten Anrede im Afrikaans und im älteren Deutsch. – *GermL* 206-209, 2010, 395-426 | E. ab.

5. STYLISTICS

320   Breed, Adri: Die hedetyd is iets van die verlede : 'n taalkundige motivering vir die 'hedetydskryfkunstradisie' in Afrikaans. – *Literator* 34/2, 2013, 9 p. | The present is a thing of the past : possible linguistic motivations for the 'present tense writing tradition' in Afrikaans prose | E. & Afrikaans ab.

321   Hendricks, Frank: Op die taalspore van S. V. Petersen : 'n blik op sy verrekening van taaldiversiteit. – *TNA* 17/2, 2010, 21-37 | [On the language tracks of S. V. Petersen : a look at his translation of language diversity] | E. ab.

7. TRANSLATION

322   Du Preez, Erica S.; Naudé, Jacobus A.: The culture-specific nature of headlines in *Finansies & tegniek* and *Finance week*. – *SALALS* 26/4, 2008, 513-523.

323   Murdoch, Alan: Strategies used in the translation of fixed expressions in magazines : a comparison of selected texts with Afrikaans as source language and South African English as target language. – *Literator* 38/2, 2017, 9 p | E. & Afrikaans ab.

324   Naudé, Jacobus A.: The role of pseudo-translations in early Afrikaans travel writing. – *SALALS* 26/1, 2008, 97-106.

325   [Neethling, Siebert J.] Neethling, Bertie: Challenges in translating RL Peteni's Xhosa novel *Kwazidenge* into Afrikaans. – *SAfrJAL* 36/1, 2016, 103-108.

326   Vyver, Corné van der: Die oorsetting van 'n bybelteks na Niestandaardafrikaans : die kunssinnigheids- en kreatiewe aspekte daaragter. – *TsGw* 51/3, 2011, 289-303 | E. ab.: The intralingual translation or rewording of a bible text into non-standard Afrikaans : the artistic and creative aspects behind it.

7.1. MACHINE TRANSLATION

327   Ehlers, Leandra; Hanekom, Gert van der Merwe: An overview of the EtsaTrans machine translation system : compilation of an administrative domain. – *Literator* 29/1, 2008, 231-247 | E. & Afrikaans ab.

328 Lotz, Susan; Rensburg, Alta van: Omission and other sins : tracking the quality of online machine translation output over four years. – *SPIL* 46, 2016, 77-97 | E. ab.

329 Lotz, Susan; Rensburg, Alta van: Translation technology explored : has a three-year maturation period done Google Translate any good? – *SPILPLUS* 43, 2014, 235-259 | E. ab.

8. SCRIPT, ORTHOGRAPHY

330 Kotzé, Ernst F.: Arabic Afrikaans – early standardisation of Afrikaans orthography : a discussion of *The Afrikaans of the Cape muslims* by Achmat Davids. – *SALALS* 30/3, 2012, 413-427 | Rev. art. of 501.

8.1. ORTHOGRAPHY

331 Alberts, Mariëtta: The Afrikaans orthographic rules as guide for other South African languages. – *Lexikos* 23, 2013, 1-28 | E. & Afrikaans ab.

332 McLachlan, J. D. (Tom): Oor die skryfwyse van Afrikaans I. – *TsGw* 56/4-2, 2016, 1280-1282 | [On the spelling of Afrikaans I].

333 McLachlan, J. D. (Tom): Oor die skryfwyse van Afrikaans II. – *TsGw* 57/1, 2017, 227-229 | [On the spelling of Afrikaans II] | Cf. part I: 332.

334 McLachlan, J. D. (Tom): Oor die skryfwyse van Afrikaans III. – *TsGw* 57/2-2, 2017, 685-687 | [On the spelling of Afrikaans III] | Cf. part II: 333.

335 McLachlan, J. D. (Tom): Oor die skryfwyse van Afrikaans IV. – *TsGw* 57/4, 2017, 1109-1110 | [On the spelling of Afrikaans IV] | Cf. part III: 334.

8.2. PUNCTUATION

336 McLachlan, J. D. (Tom): Oor deeltekens en koppeltekens. – *TsGw* 57/3, 2017, 871-873 | [On division markers and connective markers].

9.2.2. LANGUAGE COMPREHENSION

337 Sousa, Diana de: Cognitive processing skills in monolingual and bilingual South African children : implications for assessment in linguistically diverse societies. – *LM* 43/1, 2012, 97-112 | E. ab.

9.3.1.   FIRST LANGUAGE ACQUISITION, CHILD LANGUAGE

338   Southwood, Frenette: Towards a dialect-neutral assessment instrument for the language skills of Afrikaans-speaking children : the role
of socioeconomic status. – *JChL* 40/2, 2013, 415-437.

9.3.1.1.   FIRST LANGUAGE ACQUISITION BY PRE-SCHOOL CHILDREN

339   Brink, Nina; Breed, Adri: Hoe jong Afrikaanssprekende kinders betek-
enis aan hul vroeë taalgebruik verbind. – *TsGw* 57/4, 2017, 1012-1036 |
The way in which young Afrikaans children connect meaning to their
early vocabulary | E. & Afrikaans ab.

9.3.1.2.   FIRST LANGUAGE ACQUISITION BY SCHOOL CHILDREN

340   Merwe, Kristin van der; Adendorff, Ralph D.: Comprehension and production of figurative language by Afrikaans-speaking children with
and without specific language impairment. – *SALALS* 30/1, 2012, 39-63.

341   Merwe, Kristin van der; Southwood, Frenette: First and second language child speakers of Afrikaans's knowledge of figurative lan-
guage. – *PerLinguam* 24/1, 2008, 45-64 | E. ab.

342   Southwood, Frenette: The presence of a primary male caregiver
affects children's language skills. – *SPIL* 39, 2010, 75-84 | E. ab.

9.3.2.   SECOND LANGUAGE ACQUISITION

343   Conradie, Simone: "Unlearning" construction types transferred from
the L1 : evidence from adult L1 Afrikaans L2 French. – *SPILPLUS* 40,
2010, 11-26 | E. ab.

9.4.   NEUROLINGUISTICS AND LANGUAGE DISORDERS

344   Theron, Janina; Conradie, Simone; Schoeman, Renata: Pragmatic
assessment of schizophrenic bilinguals' L1 and L2 use. – *SALALS* 29/4,
2011, 515-531.

354 Banga, Arina; Hanssen, Esther; Schreuder, Robert; Neijt, Anneke: How subtle differences in orthography influence conceptual interpretation. – *WL&L* 15/2, 2012, 185-208.

355 Bekker, Ian; Levon, Erez: The embedded indexical value of /s/-fronting in Afrikaans and South African English. – *Linguistics* 55/5, 2017, 1109-1139 | E. ab.

356 Blignaut, Joline; Lesch, Harold M.: 'n Ondersoek na die taalgebruik in *Son* as verteenwoordigend van Kaaps. – *SPILPLUS* 45, 2014, 19-41 | [Research of the language use in *Son* as representative of Kaaps] | Afrikaans ab.

357 Bock, Zannie: Cyber socialising : emerging genres and registers of intimacy among young South African students. – *LM* 44/2, 2013, 68-91 | E. ab.

358 Brookes, Heather; Lekgoro, Tshepiso: A social history of urban male youth varieties in Stirtonville and Vosloorus, South Africa. – *SALALS* 32/2, 2014, 149-159.

359 Carstens, Wannie A. M.: Die storie van Afrikaans : perspektiewe op die verlede, hede en toekoms. – *TNA* 20/1, 2013, 21-49 | The story of Afrikaans : perspectives on the past, the present and the future | E. ab.

360 Chariatte, Nadine: Language crossing in Greater Cape Town : narratives of gang assaults. – (644), 333-349 | E. ab.

361 Conradie, C. Jac; Coetzee, Anna E.: Afrikaans. – (155), 897-917 | On language variation.

362 Dyers, Charlyn: The conceptual evolution in linguistics : implications for the study of Kaaps. – *Multiling* 2/2, 2015, 55-64 | E. ab.

363 Francken, Eep: De kunst of de boodschap? : schrijvers in de Zuid-Afrikaanse taalstrijd. – (20), 203-217.

364 Glorie, Ingrid: "Allengs wordt de spruyt een boom" (I) : de Stellenbossche studentenvereniging "Ons Spreekuur" (1895-1919) en de taalkwestie. – *TNA* 17/1, 2010, 20-52 | ["Allengs wordt de spruyt een boom" [Slowly/gradually the shoot becomes a tree] (I): The Stellenbosch student society "Ons spreekuur" [Our debating hour/ hour to talk] and literature (1895-1919)] | Cf. part II, 365 | E. ab.

365 Glorie, Ingrid: "Allengs wordt de spruyt een boom" (II) : de Stellenbossche studentenvereniging "Ons Spreekuur" en de literatuur (1895- 1919). – *TNA* 18/1, 2011, 60-84 | "Allengs wordt de spruyt een boom" [Slowly/gradually the shoot becomes a tree] (II) : the Stellenbosch student society "Ons spreekuur" [Our debating hour/ hour to talk] and literature (1895-1919) | Cf. part I, 364 | E. ab.

366   Grebe, Heinrich Philip: *Op die keper beskou : oor die ontstaan van Afrikaans*. – Pretoria : Van Schaik, 2012. – 167 p. – (Talatala-reeks = Talatala series ; 4).

367   Hurst, Ellen; Buthelezi, Mthuli: A visual and linguistic comparison of features of Durban and Cape Town tsotsitaal. – *SALALS* 32/2, 2014, 185-197.

368   Hurst, Ellen: Metaphor in South African tsotsitaal. – *SoLS* 10/1-2, 2016, 153-175 | E. ab.

369   Kapp, Pieter: *Maties en Afrikaans : 'n besondere verhouding, 1911-2011*. – Pretoria : Protea Boekhuis, 2013. – 261 p | [Maties and Afrikaans : a special relationship, 1911-2011] | Maties is a nickname for Stellenbosch University.

370   Kirsten, Johanita: Totius en die standaardisering van vroeg-moderne Afrikaanse werkwoorde. – *TsGw* 53/1, 2013, 60-75 | Totius and the standardisation of Early Modern Afrikaans verbs | E. & Afrikaans ab.

371   Kirsten, Johanita: What is in a language : essentialism in macro-sociolinguistic research on Afrikaans. – *IJSL* 248, 2017, 159-195 | E. ab.

372   Madell, Madelynne: Schooling superdiversity : linguistic features as linguistic resources in two Manenberg classrooms in the Western Cape. – *Multiling* 2/2, 2015, 76-85.

373   Mesthrie, Rajend; Hurst, Ellen: Slang registers, code-switching and restructured urban varieties in South Africa : an analytic overview of tsotsitaals with special reference to the Cape Town variety. – *JPCL* 28/1, 2013, 103-130.

374   Mesthrie, Rajend: "I've been speaking Tsotsitaal all my life without knowing it" : towards a unified account of Tstotsitaals in South Africa. – (49), 95-109.

375   Odendaal, Gerda: Moet Afrikaans geherstandaardiseer word? = Should Afrikaans be restandardised? – *TsGw* 54/4, 2014, 656-674 | E. & Afrikaans ab.

376   [Otto, Anna N] Otto, Annél: Sosiolinguistiek. – (165), 311-346 | [Sociolinguistics].

377   Ribbens-Klein, Yolandi: Locality, belonging and the social meanings of Afrikaans rhotic variation in the South Cape : from patterns of frequency towards moments of meaning. – *Multiling* 4/1, 2017, 7-26 | E. ab.

378   Saal, Elvis O.: To use or not to use teenage Afrikaans in HIV prevention messages directed at Afrikaans teenagers in Pretoria. – *SPILPLUS* 41, 2012, 91-105 | E. ab.

379   Simpson, Gerda: Troeteltaal in taalkundige en leksikografiese ver- band. – (43), 227-243 | Language of endearment in linguistic and lexi- cographic context | E. & Afrikaans ab.

380   Stell, Gerald: Afrikaanse spreektaalnormen en prescriptieve Afrikaanse normen : is er genoeg ruimte voor grammaticale diver- siteit in het Standaardafrikaans? – *TsGw* 50/3, 2010, 418-444 | E. ab.: Afrikaans speech norms and prescriptive Afrikaans norms : is there enough scope for grammatical diversity in Standard Afrikaans? | E., Fr. & Afrikaans ab.

381   Stell, Gerald: Comparability of the black-white divide in the American speech community and the coloured-white divide in the Afrikaans speech community. – *AS* 87/3, 2012, 294-335.

382   Stell, Gerald: Ethnicity as an independent factor of language varia- tion across space : trends in morphosyntactic patterns in spoken Afrikaans. – (14), 231-252.

383   Stell, Gerald: Grammaticale variatie in het informele gesproken Afrikaans : standaardisatie 'from above' en standaardisatie 'from below'. – (33), 109-134 | E. ab.

384   Stell, Gerald: Is there a Namibian Afrikaans? : recent trends in gram- matical variation in Afrikaans varieties within and across Namibia's borders. – *SPILPLUS* 39, 2009, 85-105.

385   Velghe, Fie; Blommaert, Jan: Emergent new literacies and the mobile phone : informal language learning, voice and identity in a South African township. – (95), 89-111.

386   Velghe, Fie: 'Hallo hoe gaan dit. wat maak jy?' : phatic communica- tion, the mobile phone and coping strategies in a South African con- text. – *Multiling* 2/1, 2015, 10-30 | E. ab.

387   [Versteegh, Cornelis H M] Versteegh, Kees: Islamic learning in Arabic- Afrikaans between Malay model and Ottoman reform. – *Wacana* 16/2, 2015, 284-303.

388   [Versteegh, Cornelis H M] Versteegh, Kees: A remarkable document in Arabic-Afrikaans : the election pamphlet of 1884. – (3), 365-380.

389   Wal, Marijke J. van der: Standaardtalen in beweging : standaardisatie en destandaardisatie in Nederland, Vlaanderen en Zuid-Afrika. – (33), 11-26 | E. ab.

390   Williams, Quentin Emmanuel: The enregisterment of English in rap braggadocio : a study from English-Afrikaans bilingualism in Cape Town. – *ET* 28/2, 2012, 54-59.

391 Williams, Quentin Emmanuel; Stroud, Christopher: Multilingualism remixed : sampling, braggadocio and the stylisation of local voice. – *AfrS* 73/1, 2014, 124-145.

10.1.1. LANGUAGE ATTITUDES AND SOCIAL IDENTITY

392 Anthonissen, Christine: '*With English the world is more open to you*' : language shift as marker of social transformation. – *ET* 29/1, 2013, 28-35 | On South African attitudes to English and Afrikaans.

393 Beukes, Anne-Marie; Pienaar, Marné: Identities in extended Afrikaans speech communities. – *NJAS* 23/3, 2014, 120-139 | Electronic publ.

394 Bock, Zannie: Code-swiching : an appraisal resource in TCR testimonies. – *FL* 18/2, 2011, 183-209 | TCR = truth and reconciliation commission.

395 Bornman, Elirea; Pauw, J. C.; Potgieter, Petrus H.: Houdings en opinies oor moedertaalonderrig en die keuse van 'n universiteit : Afrikaanssprekende studente aan Unisa = Attitudes and opinions regarding mother-tongue education and the choice of a university : Afrikaans-speaking students at Unisa. – *TsGw* 54/4, 2014, 596-609 | E. & Afrikaans ab.

396 Bornman, Elirea; Pauw, J. C.; Potgieter, Petrus H.; Janse van Vuuren, Hermanus H.: Moedertaalonderrig, moedertaalleer en identiteit : redes vir en probleme met die keuse van Afrikaans as onderrigtaal. – *TsGw* 57/3, 2017, 724-746 | Mother-tongue education, mother-tongue learning and identity : reasons for and problems with choosing Afrikaans as the language of teaching | E. & Afrikaans ab.

397 Bornman, Elirea; Potgieter, Petrus H.; Pauw, J. C.: Taalkeuses en -opinies van Afrikaanssprekende studente aan Unisa. – *TsGw* 53/3, 2013, 361-376 | Language choices and opinions of Afrikaans-speaking students at Unisa | E. & Afrikaans ab.

398 Brookes, Heather: Urban youth languages in South Africa : a case study of Tsotsitaal in a South African township. – *AnL* 56/3-4, 2014, 356-388.

399 Cage, Ken: *Gayle : the language of kinks and queens : a history and dictionary of gay language in South Africa*. – Houghton : Jacana, 2003. – 108 p.

400 Coetzee-Van Rooy, Susan: Multilingualism and social cohesion : insights from South African students (1998, 2010, 2015). – *IJSL* 242, 2016, 239-265 | E. ab.

401   Deumert, Ana: Creole as necessity? Creole as choice? : evidence from Afrikaans historical sociolinguistics. – (50), 101-122 | E. ab.

402   Deumert, Ana: The performance of a ludic self on social network(ing) sites. – (106), 23-45.

403   Hatoss, Anikó; Rensburg, Henriette van; Starks, Donna: Finding one's own linguistic space : views on English, Afrikaans and identity in a semi-urban Australian context. – *SoLS* 5/2, 2011 (2012), 257-289.

404   Horáková, Hana: Contested language : nuwe Afrikaanse beweging in a new South Africa. – (35), 183-202.

405   Hurst, Ellen; Mesthrie, Rajend: 'When you hang out with the guys they keep you in style' : the case for considering style in descriptions of South African tsotsitaals. – *LM* 44/1, 2013, 3-20 | E. ab.

406   Kassiem, Gava: Translation and identity : translation of the Freedom Charter into Afrikaans as a case in point. – *SALALS* 35/3, 2017, 271-284 | E. ab.

407   Kotzé, Ian; Kirsten, Johanita: The heritage of a language : discourses of purism in Afrikaans historical linguistics. – *LM* 47/3, 2016, 349-371 | E. ab.

408   Le Cordeur, Michael: Die variëteite van Afrikaans as draers van identiteit : 'n sosiokulturele perspektief. – *TsGw* 51/4, 2011, 758-777 | The varieties of Afrikaans as carriers of identity : a socio-cultural perspective | E. & Afr. ab.

409   Maribe, Tebogo; Brookes, Heather: Male youth talk in the construction of black lesbian identities. – *SALALS* 32/2, 2014, 199-214.

410   Maritz, Anna P.: Black Afrikaans : an alternative use. – *Literator* 37/2, 2016, 12 p | E. & Afrikaans ab.

411   Martin, Willy: De status van het Afrikaans in Zuid-Afrika en in de Nederlandssprekende landen. – *TNA* 21/2, 2014, 95-137 | The status of Afrikaans in South Africa and in the Dutch-speaking countries | E. ab.

412   Rooy, Bertus van; Doel, Rias van den: Dutch and Afrikaans as postpluricentric languages. – *IJSL* 212, 2011, 1-22.

413   Saal, Elvis O.: Teenagers' perceptions of SMS Afrikaans in print advertisements. – *SALALS* 33/1, 2015, 1-19.

414   Senekal, Burgert: Eentaligheid, integrasie en assosiasiegerigtheid in sosiale netwerke : 'n literatuuroorsig = Monolingualism, integration and assortative mixing in social networks : a literature review. – *TsGw* 55/3, 2015, 356-372 | E. & Afrikaans ab.

415   Shaikjee, Mooniq; Milani, Tommaso M.: 'It's time for Afrikaans to go' ... or not? Language ideologies and (ir)rationality in the blogosphere. – *LM* 44/2, 2013, 92-116 | E. ab.

416   Stell, Gerald; Beyer, Herman L.: Interethnic relations and language
      variation : language use and identity negotiation among Namibian
      Coloureds and Whites in interactional settings. – *SPIL* 41, 2012, 115-139
      | E. ab.

417   Stell, Gerald: *Ethnicity and language variation : grammar and code-
      switching in the Afrikaans speech community.* – Frankfurt am Main :
      Lang, 2011. – 297 p. – (Schriften zur Afrikanistik = Research in African
      studies ; 19).

418   Stell, Gerald: Ethnicity in linguistic variation : white and coloured
      identities in Afrikaans-English code-switching. – *Pragmatics* 20/3,
      2010, 425-447.

419   Stell, Gerald; Groenewald, Gerald: 'n Perseptuele verslag van
      Afrikaans in Namibië : tussen lingua franca en sosiaal-ekslusiewe
      taal. – *TsGw* 56/4-2, 2016, 1128-1148 | A perceptual account of Afrikaans
      in Namibia : between lingua franca and socially exclusive language |
      E. & Afrikaans ab.

420   Stroud, Christopher: Linguistic citizenship as utopia. – *Multiling* 2/2,
      2015, 20-37 | Includes a case study of Kaaps.

421   Thutloa, Alfred Mautsane; Huddlestone, Kate: Afrikaans as an index
      of identity among Western Cape Coloured communities. – *SPIL* 40,
      2011, 57-73 | E. ab.

10.1.2.   LANGUAGE POLICY AND LANGUAGE PLANNING

422   Alberts, Mariëtta: Die ontwikkeling van Afrikaanse vaktaal : verlede,
      hede en toekoms. – *TsGw* 56/2-1, 2016, 314-334 | The development
      of Afrikaans technical language : past, present and future | E. &
      Afrikaans ab.

423   Alberts, Mariëtta: Prolingua se bydrae tot terminologieontwikkeling
      in Afrikaans. – *Lexikos* 27, 2017, 16-49 | Prolingua's contribution to ter-
      minology development in Afrikaans | E. & Afrikaans ab.

424   Alberts, Mariëtta: Terminology development at tertiary institutions : a
      South African perspective. – *Lexikos* 24, 2014, 1-26 | E. & Afrikaans ab.

425   Carstens, Wannie A. M.: Normatiewe taalkunde. – (165), 347-372 |
      [Normative linguistics].

426   Coller, Hennie P. van: Perspektiewe op Afrikaans as 'n taal vir univer-
      siteite. – *TsGw* 56/4-1, 2016, 998-1015 | Perspectives on Afrikaans as a
      university language | E. & Afrikaans ab.

427   Conradie, C. Jac: Het Nederlands en de standaardisering van het
      Afrikaanse werkwoordssysteem. – (33), 67-84 | E. ab.

428 Cornelius, Eleanor: An appraisal of plain language in the South African banking sector. – *SPIL* 46, 2016, 25-50 | E. ab.

429 Ferreira, Dina; Plessis, Theo du: Terminologiebestuur in Suid-Afrika : 'n ideaalmodel. – *Lexikos* 20, 2010, 621-643 | E. ab.: Terminology management in South Africa : an ideal model | E. & Afrikaans ab.

430 Giliomee, Hermann: Die troebel toekoms van die Afrikaners en Afrikaans = The current troubled state of the Afrikaners and Afrikaans. – *TsGw* 54/4, 2014, 571-595 | E. & Afrikaans ab.

431 Haron, Muhammed: Revisiting *al-Qawl al-matīn* : a sociolinguistically engineered Arabic-Afrikaans text. – (3), 343-364.

432 Kotzé, Ernst F.: Afrikaans as besitting, en die vraagstuk van herstandaardisering = Afrikaans as property, and the question of restandardisation. – *TsGw* 54/4, 2014, 635-655 | E. & Afrikaans ab.

433 Kotzé, Ernst F.: Destandaardisasie en herstandardisasie : gelyklopende prosesse in die nuwe Suid-Afrika? – (33), 153-171 | E. ab.

434 Le Cordeur, Michael: Die kwessie van Kaaps : Afrikaansonderrig op skool benodig 'n meer inklusiewe benadering = The issue of Kaaps : Afrikaans teaching at school needs a more inclusive approach. – *TsGw* 55/4, 2015, 712-728 | E. & Afrikaans ab.

435 *Mainstreaming Afrikaans : regional varieties* / Ed. by Kwesi Kwaa Prah. – Cape Town : CASAS, 2012. – 155 p. – (CASAS book series ; 89) | Papers from the symposium "Mainstreaming Afrikaans regional varieties" held at the South African Centre for the Netherlands and Flanders, 24-25 January 2011 | Cf. Afrikaans version 451.

436 McLachlan, J. D. (Tom): Standaardafrikaans, standaardspelling en die *AWS*. – *TsGw* 56/2-1, 2016, 477-501 | Standard Afrikaans, standard spelling and the Afrikaans word list and spelling rules (*AWS*) | E. & Afrikaans ab.

437 Mwepu, Dominique Ngoy: Government's contribution to the development of translation in South Africa (1910-1977). – *SALALS* 26/1, 2008, 87-96.

438 Ngwenya, Themba Lancelot: The North-West University language policy : a glimmer of hope and flashes of red lights. – *LM* 43/2, 2012, 221-239 | E. ab.

439 Noordegraaf, Jan: De bril van de taalkundige : taalbeschouwing als overdracht van culturele waarden. – (33), 49-66 | E. ab.

440 Orman, Jon: Language policy and identity conflict in relation to Afrikaans in the post-apartheid era. – (116), 59-76.

441 Orman, Jon: *Language policy and nation-building in post-apartheid South Africa*. – *LPol* – Dordrecht : Springer, 2008. – xii, 204 p. – (*LPol* ; 10).

442 Pienaar, Marné: A decline in language rights violation complaints received by PanSALB : the case of Afrikaans. – *SPIL* 38, 2008, 125-137 | PanSALB = Pan South African language board.

443 Plessis, Theodorus du: Taalbeleidshersiening aan die Universiteit van die Vrystaat, 2003–2015. – *TsGw* 56/4-1, 2016, 1048-1070 | The revision of language policy at the University of the Free State, 2003–2015 | E. & Afrikaans ab.

444 Plessis, Theodorus du: Taalbeleidshersiening en die ontplanning van Afrikaans aan die Universiteit van die Vrystaat. – *SPILPLUS* 53, 2017, 78-96 | Language policy review and the unplanning of Afrikaans at the University of the Free State | E. & Afrikaans ab.

445 Rensburg, Christo van: Ná honderd jaar : die Afrikaans van die eerste taalkommissie. – *TsGw* 57/2-1, 2017, 249-270 | After a hundred years : the Afrikaans of the first Language Commission | E. & Afrikaans ab.

446 Rensburg, Christo van: Die slag toe slim sy baas gevang het. – *SPIL* 48, 2017, 51-66 | The day when the clever arguments misfired | E. ab | On the history of the standardization of Afrikaans.

447 Stell, Gerald: Metropolitan standards and post-colonial standards : what future for the Dutch connection of Afrikaans? – (11), 115-130.

448 Steyn, J. C.: G. R. von Wielligh en die Afrikaanse taalbeweging. – *TNA* 16/2, 2009, 68-91 | [G. R. von Wielligh and the Afrikaans language movement] | E. ab.

449 Steyn, J. C.: N. P. van Wyk Louw se opvattings oor taalbewegings en die behoud van Afrikaans. – *TsGw* 56/2-1, 2016, 335-354 | N. P. van Wyk Louw's views on language movements and the maintenance of Afrikaans | E. & Afrikaans ab.

450 Steyn, J. C.: Nederlandstaliges se bydraes tot die behoud en erkenning van Afrikaans 1870-1920 = Dutch language speakers' contributions to the maintenance and recognition of Afrikaans 1870-1920. – *TsGw* 54/3, 2014, 425-445 | E. & Afrikaans ab.

451 *Veelkantiger Afrikaans : streeksvariëteite in die standaardvorming* | Redakteur Kwesi Kwaa Prah. – Cape Town : CASAS, 2012. – 156 p. – (CASAS book series ; 88) | Papers from the symposium "Mainstreaming Afrikaans regional varieties" held at the South African Centre for the Netherlands and Flanders, 24-25 January 2011 | Cf. English version 435.

452   Waal, C. S. van der: Creolisation and purity : Afrikaans language poli-
      tics in post-apartheid times. – *AfrS* 71/3, 2012, 446-463.

453   Walt, Hannes van der; Steyn, Hennie: Afrikaans as taal van onder-
      rig en leer in skole en ander onderwysinstansies : "ou" wyn in nuwe
      sakke. – *TsGw* 56/4-1, 2016, 1034-1047 | Afrikaans as language of teach-
      ing and learning in schools : a "new" approach to an "old" problem | E.
      & Afrikaans ab.

454   Walt, Johannes L. van der; Wolhuter, Charl C.: Eerste taal as onderrig-
      medium in hoër onderwys : 'n internasionale perspektief. – *TsGw* 56/
      4-1, 2016, 1016-1033 | First language as medium of instruction in higher
      education : an international perspective | E. & Afrikaans ab.

455   [Webb, Victor] Webb, Vic: Managing multilingualism in higher educa-
      tion in post-1994 South Africa. – *LM* 43/2, 2012, 202-220 | E. ab.

456   [Webb, Victor] Webb, Vic: Standaardafrikaans : 'n vurk in die pad? : 'n
      taalpolitieke perspektief. – (33), 193-214 | E. ab.

457   Williams, Michellene; Bekker, Simon: Language policy and speech
      practice in Cape Town : an exploratory public health sector study. –
      SALALS 26/1, 2008, 171-183 | On Afrikaans, Xhosa & English.

10.1.3.   LANGUAGE FOR SPECIAL PURPOSES

458   Conradie, Marthinus; Niekerk, Angelique van: The use of linguistic
      tokenism to secure brand loyalty : code-switching practices in South
      African print advertising. – *LM* 46/1, 2015, 117-138 | E. ab.

459   Plessis, Lourens du: Die wonder van grondwetmatige Afrikaans. –
      TsGw 52/3, 2012, 337-351 | The wonder of constitutionalist Afrikaans.

10.1.4.   LANGUAGE LOSS AND MAINTENANCE

460   Barkhuizen, Gary P.: Maintenance, identity and social inclusion nar-
      ratives of an Afrikaans speaker living in New Zealand. – *IJSL* 222, 2013,
      77-100.

461   Dyers, Charlyn: Language shift or maintenance? : factors determining
      the use of Afrikaans among some township youth in South Africa. –
      SPIL 38, 2008, 49-72.

462   *Globalization and language vitality : perspectives from Africa* | Ed. by
      Cécile B. Vigouroux ; Salikoko S. Mufwene. – London : Continuum,
      2008. – 272 p.

463   *Halala Afrikaans* | Daniel Hugo redakteur ; Roof Bezuidenhout ;
      et al. – Pretoria : Protea Boekhuis, 2009. – 175 p.

464   Pretorius, Laurette: Die rol van die Afrikaanse Wikipedia in die uitbou
      van Afrikaans. – *TsGw* 56/2-1, 2016, 371-390 | The role of the Afrikaans
      Wikipedia in the growth of Afrikaans | E. & Afrikaans ab.

10.2.   MULTILINGUALISM, LANGUAGE CONTACT

465   Stroud, Christopher; Mpendukana, Sibonile: Towards a material
      ethnography of linguistic landscape : multilingualism, mobility and
      space in a South African township. – *JSocL* 13/3, 2009, 363-386.

10.2.1.   MULTILINGUALISM

466   Carstens, Wannie A. M.: Meertaligheid en Afrikaans in Suid-
      Afrika : die stand van sake. – *IN* 55/3, 2017, 191-207 | [Multilingualism
      and Afrikaans in South Africa : the state of affairs].

467   Coetzee-Van Rooy, Susan: Afrikaans in contact with English : endan-
      gered language or case of exceptional bilingualism? – *IJSL* 224, 2013,
      179-207.

468   Coetzee-Van Rooy, Susan: Explaining the ordinary magic of stable
      African multilingualism in the Vaal Triangle region in South Africa. –
      JMMD 35/2, 2014, 121-138.

469   Engelbrecht, Alta: Reading between the lines : hegemonic favouring
      within language-related communities. – *SALALS* 35/1, 2017, 105-120 |
      On Flemish and Afrikaans speech communities | E. ab.

470   Gass, Kate M. van: Language contact in computer-mediated com-
      munication : Afrikaans-English code switching on internet relay chat
      (IRC). – *SALALS* 26/4, 2008, 429-444.

471   Hill, Lloyd B.: The decline of academic bilingualism in South Africa : a
      case study. – *LPol* 8/4, 2009, 327-349.

472   Keymeulen, Jacques Van: Standaardisatie en destandaardisatie bij
      Vlamingen en Afrikaners : parallellen en verschillen. – (33), 135-152 |
      E. ab.

473   Nel, Joanine; Huddlestone, Kate: Analysing Afrikaans-English bilin-
      gual children's conversational code switching. – *SPIL* 41, 2012, 29-53 |
      E. ab.

474   Stell, Gerald: Codeswitching and ethnicity : grammatical types of
      codeswitching in the Afrikaans speech community. – *IJSL* 199, 2009,
      103-128.

475   Stell, Gerald: Trends in linguistic diversity in post-independence
      Windhoek : a qualitative appraisal. – *LM* 47/3, 2016, 326-348 | E. ab.

476 Williams, Quentin Emmanuel: Youth multilingualism in South
     Africa's hip-hop culture : a metapragmatic analysis. – *SoLS* 10/1-2, 2016,
     109-133 | E. ab.

10.2.3. LANGUAGE CONTACT

477 Bredenkamp, Francois: Greek and Afrikaans : the shallowest of
     influencing. – (150), 255-268.

478 Duke, Janet: Gender reduction and loss in Germanic : the Scandinavian,
     Dutch, and Afrikaans case studies. – *GermL* 206-209, 2010, 643-672.

479 McLachlan, J. D. (Tom): Die dierbare Engels. – *TsGw* 56/2-2, 2016, 725-
     726 | [That precious English language] | On anglicisms in Afrikaans.

480 Rensburg, Christo van: 'n Perspektief op 'n periode van kontak tus-
     sen Khoi en Afrikaans. – *Literator* 34/2, 2013, 11 p | A perspective on a
     period of contact between Khoi and Afrikaans | E. & Afrikaans ab.

481 Willemyns, Roland: *Dutch : biography of a language.* – Oxford : Oxford
     UP, 2013. – xviii, 289 p.

10.4. DIALECTOLOGY

482 [Breed, Adri] Breed, Catharina Adriana; Aardt, Caro A van: Postulêre
     werkwoorde in Griekwa-Afrikaans : 'n ondersoek vanuit 'n gram-
     matikaliseringsperspektief. – *SPIL* 46, 2016, 1-24 | [Postural verbs in
     Griekwa-Afrikaans : an investigation from a grammaticalization per-
     spective] | E. & Afrikaans ab.

483 Canepari, Luciano; Cerini, Marco: *Dutch & Afrikaans pronunciation
     & accents : geo-social applications of the natural phonetics & tonetics
     method.* – München : LINCOM GmbH, 2016. – 222 p. – (LINCOM stud-
     ies in phonetics ; 10) | First edition cf. 484.

484 Canepari, Luciano; Cerini, Marco: *Dutch & Afrikaans pronunciation
     & accents : geo-social applications of the natural phonetics & tonetics
     method.* – München : LINCOM Europa, 2013. – 212 p. – (LINCOM stud-
     ies in phonetics ; 10).

10.4.1. DIALECTAL LEXICON

485 Prinsloo, Anton F.: *Annerlike Afrikaans : woordeboek van Afrikaanse
     kontreitaal.* – Pretoria : Protea Boekhuis, 2009. – 536 p.

11.   COMPARATIVE LINGUISTICS

486   Heeringa, Wilbert; Wet, Febe de; Huyssteen, Gerhard B. van: Afrikaans
      and Dutch as closely-related languages : a comparison to West
      Germanic languages and Dutch dialects. – *SPILPLUS* 47, 2015, 1-18 |
      E. ab.

487   Lenz, Alexandra N.: On the resultative-modal grammaticalisa-
      tion pathway of German GET verbs : with an outlook on Dutch and
      Afrikaans. – *TeT* 67/2, 2015, 177-209 | E. ab.

488   Olmen, Daniël van; Breed, Adri: Afrikaans as Standaard Gemiddelde
      Europees : wanneer 'n lid uit sy taalarea beweeg. – *SALALS* 33/2, 2015,
      227-246 | Afrikaans & E. ab.: Afrikaans as Standard Average European :
      when a member leaves its language area.

11.1. HISTORICAL LINGUISTICS AND LANGUAGE CHANGE

489   Besten, Hans den: Desiderata for Afrikaans historical linguistics. –
      (509), 355-374 | First publ. in Dutch, cf. 163.

490   Besten, Hans den: From Khoekhoe foreigner talk via Hottentot Dutch
      to Afrikaans : the creation of a novel grammar. – (509), 257-287 | First
      publ. in 1989.

491   Biberauer, Theresa: Competing reinforcements : when languages
      opt out of Jespersen's cycle. – (14), 3-30 | On Afrikaans & Brazilian
      Portuguese.

492   Biberauer, Theresa: Jespersen off course? : the case of contemporary
      Afrikaans negation. – (8), 91-130.

493   Biberauer, Theresa: *Nie sommer nie* : sociohistorical and formal com-
      parative considerations in the rise and maintenance of the modern
      Afrikaans negation system. – *SPILPLUS* 47, 2015, 129-174 | E. ab.

494   Carstens, Wannie A. M.; Raidt, Edith H.: *Die storie van Afrikaans uit
      Europa en van Afrika.* Deel 1. *Die Europese geskiedenis van Afrikaans* –
      Pretoria : Protea Boekhuis, 2017. – 639 p | [The story of Afrikaans from
      Europe and from Africa. Vol. 1. The European history of Afrikaans].

495   Coetzee, Andries W.: Grammatical change through lexical accumula-
      tion : voicing cooccurrence restrictions in Afrikaans. – *Language* 90/3,
      2014, 693-721.

496   Conradie, C. Jac: Afrikaans en die 17de-eeuse briewe uit die see. – *TNA*
      22/1, 2015, 3-22 | Afrikaans and 17th century letters from the sea | E. ab.

497   Conradie, C. Jac: The Dutch-Afrikaans participial prefix *ge-* : a case of
      degrammaticalization? – (14), 131-153.

498   Conradie, C. Jac; Groenewald, Gerald: Die ontstaan en vestiging van Afrikaans. – (165), 27-60 | [The origin and establishment of Afrikaans].

499   Conradie, C. Jac: Taalverandering in Afrikaans. – (165), 61-89 | [Language change in Afrikaans].

500   Conradie, C. Jac: Waar zijn de Afrikaanse mutatieven gebleven? – *AUW* 3619, *NeerlW* 24, 2014, 153-162 | [What happened to the Afrikaans mutative verbs?] | E. ab.

501   Davids, Achmat: *The Afrikaans of the Cape muslims : from 1815 to 1915* / Ed. by Hein Willemse and Suleman E. Dangor. – Pretoria : Protea Boekhuis, 2011. – 318 p. – (Talatala-reeks = Talatala series ; 3).

502   Harbert, Wayne E.: Contrastive linguistics and language change : reanalysis in Germanic relative clauses. – *LiC* 12/1, 2012, 27-46.

503   Kirsten, Johanita: Frequency effects and structural change : the Afrikaans preterite. – *SPIL* 45, 2016, 147-168 | E. ab.

504   Kirsten, Johanita: *Grammatikale veranderinge in Afrikaans van 1911 tot 2010*. – Vaaldriehoek : Noordwes Universiteit, 2016. – xvii, 314 p. | [Grammatical changes in Afrikaans from 1911 to 2010] | Afrikaans ab. p. iv-v | E. ab. p. vi-vii | Diss. at the North-West University, February 2016.

505   *Ons kom van vêr : bydraes oor bruin Afrikaanssprekendes se rol in die ontwikkeling van Afrikaans* / Redakteurs: W. A. M. Carstens & Michael le Cordeur. – [South Africa] : Naledi, 2016. – xxi, 599 p. | [We come a long way : contributions to the role of coloured Afrikaans speakers in the development of Afrikaans].

506   [Rensburg, Christo van] Rensburg, MCJ van: Khoi en Oosgrensafrikaans. – *SPILPLUS* 47, 2015, 75-97 | Khoi and Eastern border Afrikaans | E. & Afrikaans ab.

507   Rensburg, Christo van: *So kry ons Afrikaans*. – Pretoria : Lapa, 2012. – 159 p.

508   Rensburg, Christo van: Die vroegste Khoi-Afrikaans. – *TsGw* 56/2-1, 2016, 454-476 | The earliest Khoi Afrikaans | E. & Afrikaans ab.

509   *Roots of Afrikaans : selected writings of Hans den Besten[1948-2010]* / Ed. by Ton van der Wouden. – Amsterdam : Benjamins, 2012. – vii, 458 p. – (Creole language library ; 44) | Posthumous publ. of articles, some publ. earlier, with additional papers by other authors.

12.2.   STATISTICAL AND QUANTITATIVE LINGUISTICS

510   Jansen, Carel; Richards, Rose; Zyl, Liezl van: Evaluating four readability formulas for Afrikaans. – *SPILPLUS* 53, 2017, 149-166 | E. ab.

14.3.5. English

522 *Communities of practice in the history of English* / Ed. by Joanna Kopaczyk ; Andreas H. Jucker. – Amsterdam : Benjamins, 2013. – vii, 291 p. – (Pragmatics & beyond. N.S. ; 235).

523 *Corpus linguistics on the move : exploring and understanding English through corpora* / Edited by María José López-Couso, Belén Méndez-Naya, Paloma Núñez-Pertejo, and Ignacio M. Palacios-Martínez. – Leiden; Boston : Brill Rodopi, 2016. – xxii, 368 p. – (Language and computers. Studies in digital linguistics ; 79).

524 *The Oxford handbook of the history of English* / Ed. by Terttu Nevalainen and Elizabeth Closs Traugott. – Oxford : Oxford UP, 2012. – xxxix, 942 p. – (Oxford handbooks in linguistics).

14.3.5.4. Modern English

1. PHONETICS AND PHONOLOGY

525 Brozbă, Gabriela: On the variability of vocalic inventory in Black South African English. – (139), 45-60, fig | E. ab.

1. PHONETICS AND PHONOLOGY

526 Bekker, Ian: Nursing the cure : a phonetic analysis of /ʊə/ in South African English. – *SPILPLUS* 42, 2013, 1-39 | E. ab.

527 Bekker, Ian: The weak vowels of South African English : a critical review and comparative acoustic analysis. – *SALALS* 32/1, 2014, 133-147.

528 Mesthrie, Rajend: Deracialising the GOOSE vowel in South African English : accelerated linguistic change amongst young, middle class females in post-apartheid South Africa. – (36), 3-18.

529 O'Grady, Cathleen; Bekker, Ian: Dentalisation as regional indicator in General South African English : an acoustic analysis of /z/, /d/ and /t/. – *SALALS* 29/1, 2011, 77-88.

530 Zerbian, Sabine: Prosodic marking of narrow focus across varieties of South African English. – *EWW* 34/1, 2013, 26-47.

1.2. PHONOLOGY

531 Bekker, Ian: The KIT-split in South African English : a critical review. – *SALALS* 32/1, 2014, 113-131.

532   Mesthrie, Rajend: Socio-phonetics and social change : deracialisation
       of the GOOSE vowel in South African English. – *JSocL* 14/1, 2010, 3-33.

1.2.1.   SUPRASEGMENTAL PHONOLOGY (PROSODY)

533   Swerts, Marc; Zerbian, Sabine: Intonational differences between L1
       and L2 English in South Africa. – *Phonetica* 67/3, 2010, 127-146 | L2
       speakers of English have Zulu as L1.

534   Zerbian, Sabine: Perception and interpretation of intonational promi-
       nence in varieties of South African English. – (19), 335-348.

2.   GRAMMAR, MORPHOSYNTAX

535   *Re-assessing the present perfect* | Ed. by Valentin Werner ; Elena
       Seoane ; Cristina Suárez-Gómez. – Berlin : De Gruyter Mouton, 2016. –
       ix, 353 p. – (Topics in English linguistics ; 91).

2.2.   SYNTAX

536   Botha, Yolande: Corpus evidence of anti-deletion in Black South
       African English noun phrases. – *ET* 29/1, 2013, 16-21.

537   [Merwe, Christian H J van der] Merwe, Christo H. J. van der: Left
       Dislocation and its translation in some Germanic languages. –
       SPILPLUS 50, 2016, 159-184 | E. ab.

538   Mesthrie, Rajend: Deletions, antideletions and complexity theory,
       with special reference to Black South African and Singaporean
       Englishes. – (17), 90-100.

539   Vos, Mark de: Atomic homogeneity : a semantic strategy for the deter-
       mination of plurality in the complex noun phrases of South African
       English. – *SALALS* 32/1, 2014, 1-19.

540   Zerbian, Sabine: Syntactic and prosodic focus marking in contact
       varieties of South African English. – *EWW* 36/2, 2015, 228-258.

3.2.   LEXICOGRAPHY

541   Mesthrie, Rajend: *A dictionary of South African Indian English.* – Cape
       Town : UCT Press, 2010. – xxviii, 260 p.

542   Otlogetswe, Thapelo Joseph; Ramaeba, Goabilwe: Developing a cam-
       pus slang dictionary for the University of Botswana. – *Lexikos* 24, 2014,
       350-361 | E. & Afrikaans ab.

3.2.1.   MONOLINGUAL LEXICOGRAPHY

543   Hicks, Sheila: Firming up the foundations : reflections on verifying the quotations in a historical dictionary, with reference to *A dictionary of South African English on historical principles*. – *Lexikos* 20, 2010, 248-271 | E. & Afrikaans ab.

544   Hiles, Lorna: Towards a Southern African English defining vocabulary. – *Lexikos* 24, 2014, 178-185 | E. & Afrikaans ab.

545   Mesthrie, Rajend: Where does a New English dictionary stop? : on the making of the *Dictionary of South African Indian English*. – *ET* 29/1, 2013, 36-43.

546   Plessis, André du; Niekerk, Tim van: Adapting a historical dictionary for the modern online user : the case of the *Dictionary of South African English on historical principles*'s presentation and navigation features. – *Lexikos* 26, 2016, 82-102 | E. & Afrikaans ab.

3.3.   ETYMOLOGY

547   Scott-Macnab, David: The treatment of *assagai* and *zagaie* by the *OED*, and of *assegai* by the *Dictionary of South African English*. – *Nph* 96/1, 2012, 151-163.

4.1.1.   LEXICAL SEMANTICS

548   Callies, Marcus: Widening the goalposts of cognitive metaphor research. – (63), 57-81 | On sports metaphors in varieties of English.

549   Malan, Saskia: Conceptual metaphors in South African political speeches (1994-2001). – *SPIL* 38, 2008, 73-106.

4.1.2.   GRAMMATICAL SEMANTICS

550   Rooy, Bertus van; Piotrowska, Caroline: The development of an extended time period meaning of the progressive in Black South African English. – (626), 465-483.

551   Rooy, Bertus van; Wasserman, Ronel: Do the modals of Black and White South African English converge? – *JEL* 42/1, 2014, 51-67.

552   Wasserman, Ronel; Rooy, Bertus van: The development of modals of obligation and necessity in White South African English through contact with Afrikaans. – *JEL* 42/1, 2014, 31-50.

4.2. PRAGMATICS, DISCOURSE ANALYSIS AND TEXT GRAMMAR

553 Adendorff, Ralph D.; Pienaar, Kiran: 'Busty babes and passionate pleasures' : a systemic functional linguistic analysis of sex worker discourse in a South African city. – (88), 31-54.

554 Huddlestone, Kate; Fairhurst, Melanie: The pragmatic markers *anyway*, *okay*, and *shame* : a South African English corpus study. – *SPILPLUS* 42, 2013, 93-110 | E. ab.

555 Senkbeil, Karsten: Figurative language in intercultural communication : a case study of German-Southern African international academic discourse. – *IPRG* 14/4, 2017, 465-491 | E. ab.

556 Siebörger, Ian; Adendorff, Ralph D.: Newspaper literacy and communication for democracy : is there a crisis in South African journalism? – *SALALS* 27/4, 2009, 413-438.

557 Siebörger, Ian; Adendorff, Ralph D.: We're talking about semantics here : axiological condensation in the South African parliament. – *FL* 24/2, 2017, 196-233 | E. ab.

558 Włodarczyk, Matylda: Infinitives in the 1820 Settler letters of denunciation : what can a contextualised application of corpus-based results tell us about the expression of persuasion? – *PSiCL* 46/4, 2010, 533-564.

559 Włodarczyk, Matylda: 1820 settler petitions in the Cape Colony : genre dynamics and materiality. – *JHP* 14/1, 2013, 45-69.

9.2.2.1. PSYCHOLOGY OF READING

560 Pretorius, Elizabeth J.; Spaull, Nic: Exploring relationships between oral reading fluency and reading comprehension amongst English second language readers in South Africa. – *RaW* 29/7, 2016, 1449-1471 | E. ab.

9.2.3. MEMORY

561 Cockroft, Kate; Alloway, Tracy: Phonological awareness and working memory : comparisons between South African and British children. – *SALALS* 30/1, 2012, 13-24 | An experiment with L1 English-speaking

children, and bilingual children speaking a Sotho or Nguni lg. and English.

9.3. LANGUAGE ACQUISITION

562 Bylund, Emanuel; Athanasopoulos, Panos: Motion event categorisation in a nativised variety of South African English. – *IJBEB* 18/5, 2015, 588-601 | E. ab.

563 *Universal or diverse paths to English phonology* / Ed. by Ulrike Gut ; Robert Fuchs ; Eva-Maria Wunder. – Berlin : De Gruyter Mouton, 2015. – v, 250 p. – (Topics in English linguistics ; 86).

9.3.1.2. FIRST LANGUAGE ACQUISITION BY SCHOOL CHILDREN

564 Willenberg, Ingrid: 'Once upon a time in Bearland' : longitudinal development of fictional narratives in South African children. – *FLang* 37/2, 2017, 150-167 | E. ab.

9.3.2. SECOND LANGUAGE ACQUISITION

565 Scheepers, Ruth: South African students' use of delexical multiword units : the trouble with high-frequency verbs. – *SPIL* 47, 2017, 89-114 | E. ab.

566 Zonneveld, Wim: Default, non-default, markedness and complexity in the L2 English word stress competence of L1 speakers of Setswana. – *SALALS* 28/4, 2010, 375-391 | On English, Afrikaans & Setswana.

9.3.2.2. GUIDED SECOND LANGUAGE ACQUISITION

567 Partridge, Maristi: A comparison of lexical specificity in the communication verbs of L1 English and TE student writing. – *SALALS* 29/2, 2011, 135-147.

10. SOCIOLINGUISTICS AND DIALECTOLOGY

568 Biberauer, Theresa; Heukelum, Marie-Louise van; Duke, Lalia: *Ja-nee. No, I'm fine'* : a note on YES and NO in South Africa. – *SPIL* 48, 2017, 67-86 | E. ab.

569   Elsness, Johan: English in South Africa : the case of past-referring verb
      forms. – (523), 181-203 | E. ab.

570   *The evolution of Englishes : the dynamic model and beyond* | Ed. by
      Sarah Buschfeld ; Thomas Hoffmann ; Magnus Huber ; Alexander
      Kautzsch. – Amsterdam : Benjamins, 2014. – xviii, 513 p. – (Varieties of
      English around the world ; G49) | In honour of Edgar Schneider on the
      occasion of his 60th birthday.

571   Mesthrie, Rajend: English in India and South Africa : comparisons,
      commonalities and contrasts. – *AfrS* 74/2, 2015, 186-198.

572   Plessis, Deon du; Bekker, Ian: 'To err is human' : the case for neorhotic-
      ity in White South African English. – *LM* 45/1, 2014, 23-39 | E. ab.

573   Siebers, Lucia: *Morphosyntax in Black South African English : a socio-
      linguistic analysis of Xhosa English.* – Tübingen : Narr, 2011. – 256 p. –
      (Language in performance ; 45).

574   *The variability of current World Englishes* | Ed. by Eugene Green and
      Charles F. Meyer. – Berlin : De Gruyter Mouton, 2014. – viii, 287 p. –
      (Topics in English linguistics ; 87/1).

575   Vos, Mark de: Homogeneity in subject-verb concord in South African
      English. – *LM* 44/1, 2013, 58-77 | E. ab.

576   Zerbian, Sabine: Prosodic marking of focus in transitive sentences in
      varieties of South African English. – (563), 209-240.

10.1.   SOCIOLINGUISTICS

577   Bekker, Ian: South African English as a *late* 19th-century extraterrito-
      rial variety. – *EWW* 33/2, 2012, 127-146.

578   Collins, James: Dilemmas of race, register, and inequality in South
      Africa. – *LiS* 46/1, 2017, 39-56 | E. ab.

579   Deumert, Ana; Mabandla, Nkululeko: 'Every day a new shop pops up' :
      South Africa's 'new' Chinese diaspora and the multilingual transfor-
      mation of rural towns. – *ET* 29/1, 2013, 44-52.

580   *English in the Indian diaspora* | Ed. by Marianne Hundt ; Devyani
      Sharma. – Amsterdam : Benjamins, 2014. – ix, 244 p. – (Varieties of
      English around the world ; G50).

581   Hartmann, Dieter; Zerbian, Sabine: Rhoticity in Black South African
      English - a sociolinguistic study. – *SALALS* 27/2, 2009, 135-148.

582   Jansen, Carel: 'Don't be a fool, put a condom on your tool' : effecten
      van retorische figuren in hiv/aids-voorlichtingsmateriaal in Zuid-
      Afrika. – *IN* 49/2, 2011, 103-116 | 'Don't be a fool, put a condom on your

tool' : the effects of rhetoric figures in HIV/AIDS educational materials in South Africa | E. ab.

583   Mesthrie, Rajend; Chevalier, Alida: Sociophonetics and the Indian diaspora : the NURSE vowel and other selected features in South African Indian English. – (580), 85-104.

584   Mesthrie, Rajend: Class, gender, and substrate erasure in sociolinguistic change : a sociophonetic study of schwa in deracializing South African English. – *Language* 93/2, 2017, 314-346 | E. ab | Incl. web-only supplemental material.

585   Mesthrie, Rajend: Ethnicity, substrate and place : the dynamics of Coloured and Indian English in five South African cities in relation to the variable (t). – *LVC* 24/3, 2012, 371-395 | On realizations of /t/ and /θ/

586   Mesthrie, Rajend: A lesser globalisation : a sociolexical study of Indian Englishes in diaspora, with a primary focus on South Africa. – (580), 171-186.

587   Minow, Verena: *Variation in the grammar of Black South African English.* – Frankfurt am Main : Lang, 2010. – xii, 266 p. – (Europäische Hochschulschriften. Reihe 21: Linguistik ; 362).

588   Rooy, Bertus van: Present perfect and past tense in Black South African English. – (535), 149-168 | E. ab.

589   Toefy, Tracey: Revisiting the kit-split in Coloured South African English. – *EWW* 38/3, 2017, 336-363 | E. ab.

590   *Varieties of English in writing : the written word as linguistic evidence* / Ed. by Raymond Hickey. – Amsterdam : Benjamins, 2010. – x, 378 p. – (Varieties of English around the world ; G41).

591   Wilmot, Kirstin: "Coconuts" and the middle-class. – *EWW* 35/3, 2014, 306-337.

592   Włodarczyk, Matylda: Community or communities of practice? : 1820 petitioners in the Cape Colony. – (522), 83-102.

10.1.1.   LANGUAGE ATTITUDES AND SOCIAL IDENTITY

593   Álvarez-Mosquera, Pedro: The use of the Implicit Association Test (IAT) for sociolinguistic purposes in South Africa. – *LM* 48/2, 2017, 69-90 | E. ab.

594   Antia, Bassey Edem; Dyers, Charlyn: Epistemological access through lecture materials in multiple modes and language varieties : the role of ideologies and multilingual literacy practices in student evaluations of such materials at a South African University. – *LPol* 15/4, 2016, 525-545 | E. ab.

595   Chariatte, Nadine: Identity construction through phonetic crossing among young Capetonian gang members. – *SoLS* 10/1-2, 2016, 45-66.

596   Coetzee-Van Rooy, Susan: The identity issue in bi- and multilingual repertoires in South Africa : implications for Schneider's dynamic model. – (570), 39-57.

597   McCormick, Tracey Lee: A queer analysis of the discursive construction of gay identity in *Gayle : the language of kinks and queens: a history and dictionary of gay language in South Africa (2003)*. – *SALALS* 27/2, 2009, 149-161 | Cf. 399.

598   McKinney, Carolyn: Orientations to English in post-apartheid schooling. – *ET* 29/1, 2013, 22-27.

599   Mesthrie, Rajend; Chevalier, Alida; McLachlan, Kate: A perception test for the deracialisation of middle class South African English. – *SALALS* 33/4, 2015, 391-409.

600   Mesthrie, Rajend: The sociophonetic effects of event X : post-apartheid Black South African English in multicultural contact with other South African Englishes. – (570), 58-69.

601   Parmegiani, Andrea: The (dis)ownership of English : language and identity construction among Zulu students at the University of KwaZulu-Natal. – *IJBEB* 17/6, 2014, 683-694 | E. ab.

10.1.2.   LANGUAGE POLICY AND LANGUAGE PLANNING

602   Banda, Felix: Defying monolingual education : alternative bilingual discourse practices in selected coloured schools in Cape Town. – *JMMD* 31/3, 2010, 221-235.

603   Drummond, Andrew: An analysis of language policy versus practice in two South African universities. – *SALALS* 34/1, 2016, 71-79 | E. ab.

604   Hibbert, Liesel: Local and global perspectives on overcoming literacy challenges in South Africa. – *IJSL* 206, 2010, 207-226.

605   Ndhlovu, Finex: Beyond neo-liberal instructional models : why multilingual instruction matters for South African skills development. – *IJLS* 7/3, 2013, 33-58.

606   Olivier, Jako: Kom *join* die PUK : die gebruik van Engels in honneursprogramme op 'n Afrikaanse universiteitskampus van die NWU = Come join the PUK : the use of English in honours programmes at an Afrikaans university campus of the NWU. – *TsGw* 54/4, 2014, 610-634 | E. & Afrikaans ab.

607   Rooy, Bertus van; Coetzee-Van Rooy, Susan: The language issue and academic performance at a South African University. – *SALALS* 33/1, 2015, 31-46.

10.1.3.   LANGUAGE FOR SPECIAL PURPOSES

608   Coertze, Salome; Conradie, Simone; Burger, Chris R.; Huddlestone, Kate: Aviation English in South African airspace. – *SPILPLUS* 42, 2013, 41-62 | E. ab.

10.2.1.   MULTILINGUALISM

609   Buschfeld, Sarah; Kautzsch, Alexander: English in Namibia : a first approach. – *EWW* 25/2, 2014, 121-160.

610   Deumert, Ana; Masinyana, Sibabalwe Oscar: Mobile language choices : the use of English and isiXhosa in text messages (SMS) : evidence from a bilingual South African sample. – *EWW* 29/2, 2008, 117-147.

611   Deumert, Ana: Tracking the demographics of (urban) language shift : an analysis of South African census data. – *JMMD* 31/1, 2010, 13-35.

612   Dyers, Charlyn: Truncated multilingualism or language shift? : an examination of language use in intimate domains in a new non-racial working class township in South Africa. – *JMMD* 29/2, 2008, 110-126 | On the use of English, Afrikaans and Xhosa.

613   McCormick, Kay M.: Polarizing and blending : compatible practices in a bilingual urban community in Cape Town. – (639), 191-209.

10.2.3.   LANGUAGE CONTACT

614   Bekker, Ian: The formation of South African English. – *ET* 29/1, 2013, 3-9.

615   Deumert, Ana; Mesthrie, Rajend: Contact in the African area : a Southern African perspective. – (524), 549-559 | E. ab.

616   Kruger, Haidee; Rooy, Bertus van: Syntactic and pragmatic transfer effects in reported-speech constructions in three contact varieties of English influenced by Afrikaans. – *LS* 56, 2016, 118-131.

617   Mesthrie, Rajend: Contact and African Englishes. – (138), 518-537.

618   Mesthrie, Rajend: A robust, living substratum : contact and socio-linguistic factors in the evolution of a variety of Black English in Kimberley, South Africa. – (574), 127-146.

619   Rooy, Bertus van: Convergence and endonormativity at phase 4 of the dynamic model. – (570), 21-38.

620   Wasserman, Ronel: *Moet* en *must* : 'n geval van Afrikaanse invloed op Suid-Afrikaanse Engels. – *TsGw* 56/1, 2016, 25-44 | *Moet* and *must* : a case of Afrikaans influence on South African English | E. & Afrikaans ab.

10.3.   LINGUISTIC GEOGRAPHY

   621   *Areal features of the Anglophone world* / Ed. by Raymond Hickey. –
        Berlin : De Gruyter Mouton, 2012. – viii, 502 p. – (Topics in English
        linguistics ; 80).

10.4.   DIALECTOLOGY

   622   Mesthrie, Rajend; Chevalier, Alida; Dunne, Timothy: A regional and
        social dialectology of the BATH vowel in South African English. – *LVC*
        27/1, 2015, 1-30.
   623   Rooy, Bertus van: A multidimensional analysis of student writing in
        Black South African English. – *EWW* 29/3, 2008, 268-305.
   624   Rooy, Bertus van; Terblanche, Lize: Complexity in word-formation
        processes in new varieties of South African English. – *SALALS* 28/4,
        2010, 357-374.

11.   COMPARATIVE LINGUISTICS

   625   Sharma, Devyani: Shared features in New Englishes. – (621), 211-232.

11.1.   HISTORICAL LINGUISTICS AND LANGUAGE CHANGE

   626   *Grammatical change in English world-wide* / Ed. by Peter Collins. –
        Amsterdam : Benjamins, 2015. – vi, 488 p. – (Studies in corpus linguis-
        tics ; 67).
   627   Rossouw, Ronel; Rooy, Bertus van: Diachronic changes in modality in
        South African English. – *EWW* 33/1, 2012, 1-26.
   628   Siebers, Lucia: 'An abundant harvest to the philologer'? : Jeremiah
        Goldswain, Thomas Shone and nineteenth-century South African
        English. – (590), 263-294 | Based on Jeremiah Goldswain's chronicle
        (1820) and the journal of Thomas Shone (1784-1868), both settlers in
        South Africa.

12.3.   STATISTICAL AND QUANTITATIVE LINGUISTICS

   629   Brato, Thorsten; Huber, Magnus: English in Africa. – (621), 161-185.
   630   Rooy, Bertus van: Corpus linguistic work on Black South African
        English. – *ET* 29/1, 2013, 10-15.

Languages of Mainland Southeast Asia

1. Sino-Tibetan

1.2. Sinitic (Chinese)

1.2.2. Modern Chinese

631   Yu, Ke; Vivier, Elmé: Speaking or being Chinese : the case of South African-born Chinese. – *IJSL* 236, 2015, 55-73.

Languages of Sub-Saharan Africa

632 *African languages and language practice research in the 21st century : interdisciplinary themes and perspectives* / Editors: Monwabisi K. Ralarala ; Ken Barris ; Eunice Ivala ; Sibawu Siyepu. – Cape Town : CASAS, 2017. – xviii, 378 p. – (CASAS book series ; 122).

633 *Africa's endangered languages : documentary and theoretical approaches* / Edited by Jason Kandybowicz ; Harold Torrence. – Oxford : Oxford University Press, 2017. – x, 520 p.

634 Banda, Felix: Language policy and orthographic harmonization across linguistic, ethnic and national boundaries in Southern Africa. – *LPol* 15/3, 2016, 257-275 | E. ab.

635 Brenzinger, Matthias: Blood becomes money : lexical acculturation in Southern Africa. – (48), 37-71.

636 *Gender and language in sub-Saharan Africa : tradition, struggle and change* / Ed. by Lilian Lem Atanga ; Sibonile Edith Ellece ; Lia Litosseliti ; Jane Sunderland. – Amsterdam : Benjamins, 2013. – xi, 331 p. – (Impact. Studies in language and society ; 33).

637 *Intonation in African tone languages* / Ed. by Laura J. Downing and Annie Rialland. – Berlin : De Gruyter Mouton, 2017. – iv, 442 p. – (Phonology and phonetics ; 24).

638 Kwamwangamalu, Nkonko M.: Multilingualism in Southern Africa. – (128), 791-812.

639 *The languages of urban Africa* / Ed. by Fiona Mc Laughlin. – London : Continuum, 2009. – x, 238 p. – (Advances in sociolinguistics).

640 Lubinga, Elizabeth: Exploring the possibility of including African proverbs in HIV and AIDS messages to influence reception by the South African youth. – *SAfrJAL* 34/Suppl., 2014, 15-22.

641 Ndhlovu, Finex: Cross-border languages in Southern African economic and political integration. – *AfrS* 72/1, 2013, 19-40.

642 Phaahla, Pinkie: Indigenous African languages as agents of change in the transformation of higher education institutions in South Africa : Unisa. – *NJAS* 23/1, 2014, 31-56 | Electronic publ.

643   Raselekoane, Nanga Raymond: African languages and the challenges
       of community development in South Africa. – *SAfrJAL* 34/Suppl.,
       2014, 1-8.

644   *Sociolinguistics in African contexts : perspectives and challenges* /
       Augustin Emmanuel Ebongue ; Ellen Hurst, editors. – Cham : Springer,
       2017. – viii, 349 p. – (Multilingual education ; 20) | Not analyzed.

1.   Niger-Congo (Niger-Kordofanian)

1.7.   Benue-Congo

645   Bennett, William: Agreement, history, and Obolo : a reply to Connell. –
       SPILPLUS 48, 2015, 13-15 | Reply to 183.

1.7.1.   Bantu

646   *Bantu languages : analyses, description and theory* / Ed. by Karsten
       Legère ; Christina Thornell. – Köln : Köppe, 2011. – xiv, 347 p. – (East
       African languages and dialects ; 20).

647   Seidel, Frank: *A grammar of Yeyi : a Bantu language of Southern
       Africa.* – Köln : Köppe, 2008. – 464 p. – (Grammatische Analysen afri-
       kanischer Sprachen = Grammatical analyses of African languages ;
       33).

0.5.   SEMIOTICS

648   Dowling, Tessa: '*Akuchanywa apha please*' No peeing here please : the
       language of signage in Cape Town. – *SAfrJAL* 30/2, 2010, 192-208.

0.6.   APPLIED LINGUISTICS

649   Marten, Lutz; Mostert, Carola: Background languages, learner motiva-
       tion and self-assessed progress in learning Zulu as an additional lan-
       guage in the UK. – *IJM* 9/1, 2012, 101-128 | E. ab.

650   Mayaba, N. N.: Strategy to improve a conversational isiXhosa module :
       insights gained from 'out-of-class' experiences of Foundation phase
       English/Afrikaans students. – *SAfrJAL* 36/2, 2016, 133-140.

651   Nkomo, Dion: Beyond meaning in dictionaries : teaching Ndebele
       grammar using *Isichazamazwi SesiNdebele.* – *SAfrJAL* 29/1, 2009,
       30-42.

652   Otlogetswe, Thapelo Joseph: The design of Setswana Scrabble. –
      SAfrJAL 36/2, 2016, 153-161.

653   Scaraffiotti, Zamantuli: *Parlons Xhosa : Afrique du Sud.* – Paris :
      L'Harmattan, 2011. – 158 p. – (Parlons).

1.   PHONETICS AND PHONOLOGY

654   Bennett, William G.; Diemer, Maxine; Kerford, Justine; Probert, Tracy;
      Wesi, Tsholofelo: Setswana (South African). – *JIPA* 46/2, 2016, 235-246
      | Illustrations of the IPA.

655   Doke, Clement M.: *The phonetics of the Zulu language.* – München :
      LINCOM Europa, 2012. – 310 p. – (LINCOM gramatica ; 166).

656   Gxowa-Dlayedwa, Ntombizodwa Cynthia: Ukufundisa izicuku
      zeziqhakancu emagameni. – *PerLinguam* 31/3, 2015, 32-48 | Teaching
      click clusters in words | E. & Xhosa ab.

657   Naidoo, Shamila: A re-evaluation of the Zulu implosive [ɓ]. – *SAfrJAL*
      30/1, 2010, 1-10.

658   Naidoo, Shamila; Roux, Justus C.: Integrating phonetics and pho-
      nology in the description of the intrusive stop formation process in
      Zulu. – *SAfrJAL* 28/1, 2008, 36-48.

659   Wissing, Daan P.: Aspects of the phonetics and phonology of Southern
      Sotho /a/. – *SAfrJAL* 30/2, 2010, 234-241.

1.1.   PHONETICS

660   Chen, Yiya; Downing, Laura J.: All depressors are not alike : a compari-
      son of Shanghai Chinese and Zulu. – (29), 243-265.

661   [Thomas, Kimberley D] Thomas-Vilakati, Kimberly Diane:
      Coproduction and coarticulation in Isizulu clicks. – Berkeley, CA : Univ.
      of California Press, 2010. – 258 p. – (Univ. of California publications.
      Linguistics ; 144).

1.1.1.   ARTICULATORY PHONETICS

662   Lee-Kim, Sang-Im; Kawahara, Shigeto; Lee, Seunghun J.: The 'whis-
      tled' fricative in Xitsonga : its articulation and acoustics. – *Phonetica*
      71/1, 2014, 50-81.

663   Shosted, Ryan K.: Articulatory and acoustic characteristics of whistled
      fricatives in Changana. – (30), 119-129.

1.1.2. ACOUSTIC PHONETICS

664   Barnard, Etienne; Wissing, Daan P.: Vowel variation in Southern Sotho : an acoustic investigation. – *SALALS* 26/2, 2008, 255-265.

665   Boyer, One Tlale; Zsiga, Elizabeth C.: Phonological devoicing and phonetic voicing in Setswana. – (31), 82-89 | Also freely available online.

666   Le Roux, Mia: An acoustic comparison : Setswana vowels versus the cardinal vowels. – *SAfrJAL* 32/2, 2012, 175-180.

667   Le Roux, Mia; Le Roux, Jurie: An acoustic assessment of Setswana vowels. – *SAfrJAL* 28/2, 2008, 156-171.

668   Midtlyng, Patrick J.: The effects of speech rate on VOT for initial plosives and click accompaniments in Zulu. – (30), 105-118.

669   Wissing, Daan P.: Aspects of vowel raising in Southern Sotho and Setswana : an acoustic approach. – *SAfrJAL* 30/2, 2010, 242-249.

670   Wissing, Daan P.; Pienaar, Wikus: Evaluating vowel normalisation procedures : a case study on Southern Sotho vowels. – *SALALS* 32/1, 2014, 97-111.

671   Zerbian, Sabine; Barnard, Etienne: Phonetics of intonation in South African Bantu languages. – *SALALS* 26/2, 2008, 235-254.

1.1.4. SPEECH TECHNOLOGY

672   Westhuizen, Ewald van der; Niesler, Thomas: The effect of postlexical deletion on automatic speech recognition in fast spontaneously spoken Zulu. – *Interspeech*, 2016, 3559-3563 | E. ab.

1.2. PHONOLOGY

673   Coetzee, Andries W.; Pretorius, Rigardt: Phonetically grounded phonology and sound change : the case of Tswana labial plosives. – *JPhon* 38/3, 2010, 404-421.

674   Gouskova, Maria; Zsiga, Elizabeth C.; Tlale Boyer, One: Grounded constraints and the consonants of Setswana. – *Lingua* 121/15, 2011, 2120-2152.

675   Halpert, Claire: Overlap-driven consequences of nasal place assimilation. – (6), 345-368 | On Zulu.

676   Lee, Seunghun J.; Burheni, Clementinah: Repair strategies in labial dissimilation : diminutive formations in Xitsonga. – *SPILPLUS* 44, 2014, 89-103 | E. ab.

677   Malambe, Gloria B.: Mid vowel assimilation in siSwati. – *SALALS* 33/3, 2015, 261-272.

678   Vratsanos, Alyssa; Kadenge, Maxwell: Hiatus resolution in Xitsonga. – *SPILPLUS* 52, 2017, 175-196 | E. ab.

1.2.1.   SUPRASEGMENTAL PHONOLOGY (PROSODY)

679   Archer, Brent: Sonority in Zulu. – (69), 63-75.

680   Batibo, Herman M.: The evolution and adaptation of Swahili and Tswana syllable structures. – (46), 13-33.

681   Bennett, William G.; Lee, Seunghun J.: A surface constraint in Xitsonga : *li. – *AfrL* 21, 2015, 3-27 | E. & Fr. ab.

682   Downing, Laura J.: Prosodic phrasing in relative clauses : a comparative look at Zulu, Chewa and Tumbuka. – (646), 17-29.

683   Halpert, Claire: Prosody/syntax mismatches in the Zulu conjoint/disjoint alternation. – (989), 329-349.

684   Harford, Carolyn; Malambe, Gloria B.: Optimal register variation : high vowel elision in siSwati. – *SALALS* 33/3, 2015, 343-357.

685   Lee, Seunghun J.: Cumulative effects in Xitsonga : high-tone spreading and depressor consonants. – *SALALS* 33/3, 2015, 273-290.

686   McCarthy, John J.; Mullin, Kevin; Smith, Brian W.: Implications of harmonic serialism for lexical tone association. – (72), 265-297 | Evidence from Esimbi, Kikuyu, Etung and Venda.

687   Zeller, Jochen; Zerbian, Sabine; Cook, Toni: Prosodic evidence for syntactic phrasing in Zulu. – (989), 295-328.

688   Zerbian, Sabine; Barnard, Etienne: Realisations of a single high tone in Northern Sotho. – *SALALS* 27/4, 2009, 357-380.

689   Zerbian, Sabine: Morpho-phonological and morphological minimality in Tswana monosyllabic stems (Southern Bantu). – (18), 131-148.

690   Zerbian, Sabine: Onset consonants in Tswana : Cw-sequences and affricates. – (46), 143-165.

691   Zerbian, Sabine: Sentence intonation in Tswana (Sotho-Tswana group). – (637), 393-433 | E. ab.

1.3.   MOR(PHO)PHONOLOGY

692   Braver, Aaron; Bennett, William G.: Phonotactic c(l)ues to Bantu noun class disambiguation. – *LingVan* 2/1, 2016, 1-11.

693   Cook, Toni: Adjectival reduplication in Zulu. – *SALALS* 32/4, 2014, 433-446.

694   Cook, Toni: The status of the macrostem in reduplication in Ndebele and Zulu. – (26), 46-60.

695   Creissels, Denis: The conjoint/disjoint distinction in the tonal morphology of Tswana. – (989), 200-238.

696   Dube, Progress; Ndebele, Lickel: A morphophonological account of Ndebele demonstrative delimitators. – (40), 219-233.

697   Harford, Carolyn: Prosody in verbal inflection in Isizulu. – (21), 288-297.

698   Kotzé, Albert E.: Making sense of irregular realisations of the past tense suffix in Northern Sotho : the phonology-morphology interface. – SALALS 26/2, 2008, 217-234.

699   Lee, Seunghun J.: Domains of H tone spreading and the noun class prefix in Xitsonga. – SALALS 32/1, 2014, 21-34.

700   Mathonsi, Nhlanhla; Naidoo, Shamila: Imbrication triggered by the suffix -ile in isiZulu. – SAfrJAL 32/2, 2012, 167-173.

701   Monich, Irina: Tonal processes in the Setswana verb. – JALL 35/2, 2014, 141-204.

702   Spuy, Andrew van der: Bilabial palatalisation in Zulu : a morphologically conditioned phenomenon. – SPILPLUS 44, 2014, 71-87 | E. ab.

703   Zerbian, Sabine; Barnard, Etienne: Realisation of two adjacent high tones : acoustic evidence from Northern Sotho. – SALALS 28/2, 2010, 101-121.

704   Zerbian, Sabine: A guide to tones in Tswana locatives. – SAfrJAL 31/2, 2011, 254-264.

2. GRAMMAR, MORPHOSYNTAX

705   Andrason, Alexander; Dlali, Mawande: Tense and aspect of performatives in isiXhosa. – SAfrJAL 37/2, 2017, 149-161 | E. ab.

706   Baker, Anne Edith: Die Nomenklassifizierung des Zulu als positiver Transfer in DaFiA in Südafrika. – (2), 351-356 | [The noun classification of Zulu as positive transfer in DaFiA in South Africa].

707   Creissels, Denis: The 'new adjectives' of Tswana. – (75), 75-94.

708   Dowling, Tessa; Deyi, Somikazi; Whitelaw, Emma: Merger of noun classes 3 and 1 : a case study with bilingual isiXhosa-speaking youth. – SAfrJAL 37/1, 2017, 41-49 | E. ab.

709   Gxowa-Dlayedwa, Ntombizodwa Cynthia: The reflexive marker as drawn from authentic texts in isiXhosa. – SAfrJAL 31/2, 2011, 302-314.

710   Kubayi, Sikheto Joe; Madadzhe, Richard Ndwayamato: The non-derived ideophone in Xitsonga. – SAfrJAL 35/2, 2015, 261-271.

711   Lee, Seunghun J.; [Hlungwani, Madala Crous] Hlungwani, Crous: Aspectual auxiliary verbs in Xitsonga. – *SPILPLUS* 48, 2015, 113-135 | E. ab.

712   Posthumus, Lionel C.: Naming the so-called continuous past tenses of the south-eastern Bantu languages with particular reference to Zulu. – *SAfrJAL* 28/1, 2008, 69-79.

713   Posthumus, Lionel C.: Tense marking in copulatives with particular reference to isiZulu. – *SAfrJAL* 37/2, 2017, 163-172 | E. ab.

714   Pretorius, W. J.: Adverbial descriptions in Northern Sotho. – *SAfrJAL* 29/1, 2009, 20-29.

715   Taljard, Elsabé; Schryver, Gilles-Maurice de: A corpus-driven account of the noun classes and genders in Northern Sotho. – *SALALS* 34/2, 2016, 169-185 | E. ab.

716   Visser, Marianna W.: Definiteness and specificity in the isiXhosa determiner phrase. – *SAfrJAL* 28/1, 2008, 11-29.

2.1.   MORPHOLOGY AND WORD-FORMATION

717   Dube, Progress; Ndebele, Lickel; Ndlovu, Mbulisi: An analysis of the status of the secondary noun prefixes in Ndebele. – *SAfrJAL* 34/2, 2014, 145-149.

718   Gowlett, Derek F.; Dowling, Tessa: Incipient merger of Cls 11 and 5 in Xhosa? – *SAfrJAL* 35/1, 2015, 67-81.

719   Halpert, Claire; Karawani, Hadil: Aspect in counterfactuals from A(rabic) to Z(ulu). – (22), 99-107.

720   Keet, C. Maria; Khumalo, Langa: Grammar rules for the isiZulu complex verb. – *SALALS* 35/2, 2017, 183-200 | E. ab.

721   Kosch, Ingeborg M.: Descriptive issues of derivation and inflection in Sesotho sa Leboa (Northern Sotho) with particular reference to 'number'. – *SALALS* 29/1, 2011, 89-96.

722   Kotzé, Albert E.: Lexical generality as a determinant of extension position in Northern Sotho. – *SAfrJAL* 31/1, 2011, 30-40.

723   Kotzé, Petronella M.: Northern Sotho grammatical descriptions : the design of a tokeniser for the verbal segment. – *SALALS* 26/2, 2008, 197-208.

724   Kotzé, Petronella M.: Tokenization rules for the disjunctively written verbal segment of Northern Sotho. – *SAfrJAL* 31/1, 2011, 121-137.

725   Mojapelo, Mampaka: Morphology and semantics of proper names in Northern Sotho. – *SAfrJAL* 29/2, 2009, 185-194.

726   Monich, Irina: Comparative morphological analysis of the perfect form in Sesotho and isiZulu. – *NLLT* 33/4, 2015, 1271-1292 | E. ab.

727   Nichols, Peter: Persistive and alterative – dual-time aspects in siSwati. – (28), 477-487.

728   Pretorius, Rigardt: The sequence and productivity of Setswana verbal suffixes. – *SPILPLUS* 44, 2014, 49-70 | E. ab.

729   Spuy, Andrew van der: The morphology of the Zulu locative. – *TPhS* 112/1, 2014, 61-79.

730   Spuy, Andrew van der: Post-inflectional derivation in Zulu : further evidence against the split morphology hypothesis. – *LM* 44/1, 2013, 78-93.

731   Spuy, Andrew van der: Zulu noun affixes : a generative account. – *SAfrJAL* 29/2, 2009, 195-215.

732   Taraldsen, Knut Tarald: The nanosyntax of Nguni noun class prefixes and concords. – *Lingua* 120/6, 2010, 1522-1548.

2.1.1. INFLECTIONAL MORPHOLOGY

733   Marten, Lutz: The great siSwati locative shift. – (7), 249-267.

734   Spuy, Andrew van der: A construction grammar account of Zulu singular/plural inflection. – *NJAS* 26/3, 2017, 191-214 | E. ab.

735   Spuy, Andrew van der: Generation of the isiZulu subjunctive. – *SALALS* 30/1, 2012, 77-92.

736   Stump, Gregory T.: Rules and blocks. – (74), 421-439 | E. ab.

2.1.2. DERIVATIONAL MORPHOLOGY

737   Chebanne, Andy: Case system or case traces in derivational formations in Setswana? – (21), 275-287.

738   Hlungwani, Madala Crous: Intransitive psych verbs and nominalisation in Xitsonga. – *SAfrJAL* 34/Suppl., 2014, 35-41 | Within the framework of generative lexicon theory.

739   Mletshe, Loyiso: Deverbal nominals derived from intransitive state verbs in isiXhosa : a Generative Lexicon approach. – *SAfrJAL* 37/1, 2017, 29-39 | E. ab.

740   Ndlovu, Sambulo: Structural and philosophical aspects in isiNdebele retronym derivation. – *SAfrJAL* 32/2, 2012, 153-160.

2.2. SYNTAX

741 Andrason, Alexander; Visser, Marianna W.: The mosaic evolution of Left Dislocation in Xhosa. – *SPILPLUS* 50, 2016, 139-158 | E. ab.

742 Buell, Leston Chandler: Class 17 as a non-locative noun class in Zulu. – *JALL* 33/1, 2012, 1-35.

743 Buell, Leston Chandler; Dreu, Simon de: Subject raising in Zulu and the nature of PredP. – *LRev* 30/3, 2013, 423-466 | E. ab.

744 Buell, Leston Chandler: VP-internal DPs and right-dislocation in Zulu. – *LIN* 25, 2008, 37-49.

745 Buell, Leston Chandler: Zulu *ngani* 'why' : postverbal and yet in CP. – *Lingua* 121/5, 2011, 805-821.

746 Burkholder, Ross: The syntactic structure of negation in Ndebele. – (9), 235-254.

747 Carstens, Vicki May; Mletshe, Loyiso: Negative concord and nominal licensing in Xhosa and Zulu. – *NLLT* 34/3, 2016, 761-804 | Erratum: p. 805-806 | E. ab.

748 Carstens, Vicki May; Mletshe, Loyiso: Radical defectivity : implications of Xhosa expletive constructions. – *LI* 46/2, 2015, 187-242.

749 Cheng, Lisa Lai-Shen; Downing, Laura J.: Against FocusP : arguments from Zulu. – (89), 247-266.

750 Cheng, Lisa Lai-Shen; Downing, Laura J.: Clefts in Durban Zulu. – (77), 141-163.

751 Cheng, Lisa Lai-Shen; Downing, Laura J.: The problems of adverbs in Zulu. – (68), 42-59.

752 Cheng, Lisa Lai-Shen; Downing, Laura J.: Where's the topic in Zulu? – *LRev* 26/2-3, 2009, 207-238.

753 Creissels, Denis: Additive coordination, comitative adjunction, and associative plural in Tswana. – *LLACAN* 2, 2016, 11-42 | E. & Fr. ab.

754 Creissels, Denis: Tswana locatives and their status in the inversion construction. – *AfrL* 17, 2011, 33-52.

755 Dreu, Merijn de; Buell, Leston Chandler: Neuter gender in a sexless language : the case of Zulu. – *LIN* 29, 2012, 41-54.

756 Duarte, Fábio Bonfim: Tense encoding, agreement patterns, definiteness and relativization strategies in Changana. – (30), 80-94.

757 Gibson, Hannah; Marten, Lutz: Variation and grammaticalisation in Bantu complex verbal constructions : the dynamics of information growth in Swahili, Rangi and SiSwati. – (76), 70-109.

758   Halpert, Claire: *Argument licensing and agreement.* – Oxford : Oxford UP, 2015. – xvi, 296 p. – (Oxford studies in comparative syntax) | On Zulu.

759   Halpert, Claire: Case, agreement, EPP and information structure : a quadruple-dissociation in Zulu. – (22), 90-98.

760   Halpert, Claire; Zeller, Jochen: Right dislocation and raising-to-object in Zulu. – *LRev* 32/3, 2015, 475-513 | E. ab.

761   Khumalo, Langa: Generative grammar and cognitive grammar : a case of the passive construction in Ndebele. – (40), 37-55.

762   Khumalo, Langa: On subject agreement in isiNdebele. – *SAfrJAL* 34/2, 2014, 137-143.

763   Khumalo, Langa: The passive and stative constructions in Ndebele : a comparative analysis. – *NJAS* 18/2, 2009, 154-174 | Electronic publ.

764   Khumalo, Langa: Passive, locative inversion in Ndebele and the unaccusative hypothesis. – *SAfrJAL* 30/1, 2010, 22-34.

765   Krüger, Casper J. H.: *Setswana syntax : a survey of word group structures.* 2 vols. – München : LINCOM Europa, 2013. – xxxi, 233; xxviii, 506 p. – (LINCOM studies in African linguistics ; 87-88).

766   Kubayi, Sikheto Joe: 'It' subject constructions in Xitsonga. – *SALALS* 31/1, 2013, 39-59.

767   Langa, David Alberto Seth: Negation in the past tense in Changana. – (21), 255-267.

768   Le Roux, Jurie: The border dispute between adverbials and conjunctions in Tswana grammar. – *SAfrJAL* 31/1, 2011, 54-65.

769   Lee, Seunghun J.; [Hlungwani, Madala Crous] Hlungwani, Crous: Distribution of conjunctive and disjunctive forms in Xitsonga. – *SPILPLUS* 52, 2017, 157-173 | E. ab.

770   Mojapelo, Mampaka: Re-examining the relationship between the subject agreement morpheme and (in)definiteness in Northern Sotho. – *Literator* 34/1, 2013, 8 p. | E. & Afrikaans ab.

771   Morapedi, Setumile: Focus constructions in Setswana : information structure approach. – (21), 268-274.

772   Ngunga, Armindo Saúl Atelela; Duarte, Fábio Bonfim; Camargos, Quesler Fagundes: Differential object marking in Mozambican languages. – (9), 333-353.

773   Pretorius, Rigardt; Berg, Ansu; Pretorius, Laurette: Multiple object agreement morphemes in Setswana : a computational approach. – *SALALS* 30/2, 2012, 203-218.

774   Sibanda, Galen: The Ndebele applicative construction. – (9), 309-332.

775   Ström, Eva-Marie Bloom: What the giant tells us about agreeing post-verbal subjects in Xhosa. – *SPILPLUS* 52, 2017, 73-100 | E. ab.

776   Visser, Marianna W.: Definiteness and specificity in the Xhosa determiner phrase. – (646), 295-314.

777   Vos, Mark de; Mitchley, Hazel: Subject marking and preverbal coordination in Sesotho : a perspective from optimality theory. – *SALALS* 30/2, 2012, 155-170.

778   Zeller, Jochen: Argument prominence and agreement : explaining an unexpected object asymmetry in Zulu. – *Lingua* 156, 2015, 17-39.

779   Zeller, Jochen: Instrument inversion in Zulu. – (32), 134-148.

780   Zeller, Jochen: Locative inversion in Bantu and predication. – *Linguistics* 51/6, 2013, 1107-1146.

781   Zeller, Jochen: Mobility as a feature : evidence from Zulu. – *SPILPLUS* 48, 2015, 69-92 | E. ab.

782   Zeller, Jochen: Object marking in isiZulu. – *SALALS* 30/2, 2012, 219-235.

783   Zeller, Jochen: On clitic left dislocation in Zulu. – *FAB* 18, 2006 (2009), 131-156.

3.1.   LEXICOLOGY

784   Le Roux, Jurie: Revisiting Setswana basic colour terms. – *SAfrJAL* 33/2, 2013, 159-164.

3.2.   LEXICOGRAPHY

785   Mafela, Munzhedzi James: Borrowing and dictionary compilation : the case of the indigenous South African languages. – *Lexikos* 20, 2010, 691-699 | E. & Afrikaans ab.

786   Mafela, Munzhedzi James: Proverbs as illustrative examples in a Tshivenda bilingual dictionary : a reflection of meaning and culture. – *SAfrJAL* 28/1, 2008, 30-35.

787   Mathangwane, Joyce T.: Abbreviations and acronyms : the case of *Tlhalosi ya Medi ya Setswana*. – *Lexikos* 25, 2015, 233-245 | E. & Afrikaans ab.

788   Mathonsi, Nhlanhla: A headword identification problem of nouns in Zulu dictionaries. – (646), 163-173.

789   Mojela, V. M.: Borrowing and loan words : the lemmatizing of newly acquired lexical items in Sesotho sa Leboa. – *Lexikos* 20, 2010, 700-707 | E. & Afrikaans ab.

790   Nkomo, Dion; Wababa, Zola: IsiXhosa lexicography : past, present and future. – *Lexikos* 23, 2013, 348-370 | E. & Afrikaans ab.

791   Prinsloo, D. J.; Bothma, Theo J. D.; Heid, Ulrich; Prinsloo, Daniel J.: Direct user guidance in e-dictionaries for text production and text reception : the verbal relative in Sepedi as a case study. – *Lexikos* 27, 2017, 403-426 | E. & Afrikaans ab.

792   Prinsloo, D. J.: Corpus-based lexicography for lesser-resourced languages : maximizing the limited corpus. – *Lexikos* 25, 2015, 285-300 | E. & Afrikaans ab.

793   [Schryver, Gilles Maurice] Schrijver, Gilles-Maurice de: The lexicographic treatment of quantitative pronouns in Zulu. – *Lexikos* 18, 2008, 92-105 | E. & Dutch ab.

794   Zondo, Jerry: Affirming verb lexemes in *A practical Ndebele dictionary* and in *Isichazamazwi SesiNdebele* : the case of -*wa* verbs. – *Lexikos* 19, Suppl., 2009, 166-174.

3.2.1.   MONOLINGUAL LEXICOGRAPHY

795   Khumalo, Langa: Users, user-friendliness and projected uses of *Isichazamazwi SesiNdebele* : an analysis. – *Lexikos* 19, Suppl., 2009, 16-25 | On a monolingual Ndebele dictionary.

796   Maphosa, Mandlenkosi; Nkomo, Dion: The microstructure of *Isichazamazwi SesiNdebele*. – *Lexikos* 19, Suppl., 2009, 38-50 | On a monolingual Ndebele dictionary.

797   Mphahlele, Motlokwe Clifford: The lemmatisation of dialectal forms in a Northern Sotho general monolingual dictionary : is the language developed or polluted? – (43), 155-164 | E. & Afrikaans ab.

798   Ndlovu, Eventhough: Sense relations in the treatment of meaning in *Isichazamazwi SesiNdebele*. – *Lexikos* 19, Suppl., 2009, 71-85 | On a monolingual Ndebele dictionary.

799   Ndlovu, Eventhough: The treatment of borrowed nouns in *Isichazamazwi SesiNdebele* and *Isichazamazwi SezoMculo*. – *Lexikos* 19, Suppl., 2009, 86-101 | On two monolingual Ndebele dictionaries, one general and the other of musical terms.

800   Otlogetswe, Thapelo Joseph: Introducing *Tlhalosi ya Medi ya Setswana* : the design and compilation of a monolingual Setswana dictionary. – *Lexikos* 23, 2013, 532-547 | E. & Afrikaans ab.

801   Otlogetswe, Thapelo Joseph: Treatment of spelling variants in Setswana monolingual dictionaries. – *Lexikos* 25, 2015, 262-284 | E. & Afrikaans ab.

3.2.2.   PLURILINGUAL LEXICOGRAPHY

802   Gouws, Rufus H.; [Prinsloo, D J] Prinsloo, Danie; Dlali, Mawande: A series of foundation phase dictionaries for a multilingual environment. – *SPIL* 43, 2014, 23-43 | E. ab.

803   *Isichazamazwi sesikole esinezilimi ezimbili isiZulu Nesingisi : esishicilelwe abakwa-Oxford.Oxford bilingual school dictionary : Zulu and English* / Ed. by Gilles-Maurice de Schryver ; Nomusa Sibiya [et al.]. – Cape Town : Oxford UP. Southern Africa, 2010. – lviii, 582 p.

804   Kosch, Ingeborg M.: An analysis of the *Oxford bilingual school dictionary : Northern Sotho and English* (De Schryver 2007). – *Lexikos* 23, 2013, 611-627 | Rev. art. of 816 | E. & Afrikaans ab.

805   Kosch, Ingeborg M.: Lemmatisation of fixed expressions : the case of proverbs in northern Sotho. – *Lexikos* 26, 2016, 145-161 | E. & Afrikaans ab.

806   Madiba, Mbulungeni; Nkomo, Dion: The *Tshivenḍa-English ṭhalusamaipfi/dictionary* as a product of South African lexicographic processes. – *Lexikos* 20, 2010, 307-325 | E. & Afrikaans ab.

807   Mahlangu, Sponono: The lemmatization of loan words in the *isiNdebele-English isiHlathululi-imagama/Dictionary* and their successful incorporation into the language. – *Lexikos* 24, 2014, 186-197 | E. & Afrikaans ab.

808   Mojela, V. M.: A balanced and representative corpus : the effects of strict corpus-based dictionary compilation in Sesotho sa Leboa. – *Lexikos* 23, 2013, 286-296 | E. & Afrikaans ab.

809   Mongwe, M. J.: Bilingual dictionaries in the South African context. – (43), 127-147 | E. & Afrikaans ab.

810   Nthambeleni, Mashudu; Mbulaheni Musehane, Nelson: The lemmatisation of nouns in Tshivenḍa dictionaries. – *Lexikos* 24, 2014, 214-224 | E. & Afrikaans ab.

811   Prinsloo, D. J.: A bilingual dictionary for a specific user group : supporting Setswana speakers in the production and reception of English. – *SAfrJAL* 31/1, 2011, 66-86.

812   Prinsloo, D. J.: A critical analysis of the lemmatisation of nouns and verbs in isiZulu. – *Lexikos* 21, 2011, 169-193 | E. & Afrikaans ab.

813   Prinsloo, D. J.: A critical evaluation of the paradigm approach in Sepedi lemmatisation : the *Groot Noord-Sotho woordeboek* as a case in point. – *Lexikos* 24, 2014, 251-271 | Illustrated by the verb stem -*roba* | E. & Afrikaans ab.

814   Prinsloo, D. J.: Die leksikografiese bewerking van verwantskapsterme in Sepedi. – *Lexikos* 22, 2012, 272-289 | E. ab.: The lexicographical treatment of kinship terminology in Sepedia | E. & Afrikaans ab.

815   Prinsloo, D. J.: Lexicographic treatment of kinship terms in an English/ Sepedi-Setswana-Sesotho dictionary with an amalgamated lemmalist. – *Lexikos* 24, 2014, 272-290 | E. & Afrikaans ab.

816   *Pukuntšu ya polelopedi ya sekolo : Sesotho sa Leboa le Seisimane : e gatišitšwe ke Oxford.Oxford bilingual school dictionary : Northern Sotho and English* / Ed. by G.-M. de Schryver ; M. Mogodi ; E. Taljard [et al.]. – Cape Town : Oxford UP., 2007. – xii, 552 p.

817   Schryver, Gilles-Maurice de: The lexicographic treatment of ideophones in Zulu. – *Lexikos* 19, 2009, 34-54 | On a Zulu-English lexicographic project.

818   Schryver, Gilles-Maurice de: *Oxford Isixhosa – Isingesi isichazimagama sesikolo.Oxford English – Isixhosa school dictionary* / Eds.-in-chief: Gilles-Maurice de Schryver (consulting) ; Mary Reynolds ; Isixhosa-Isingesi compilers: Fumanekile Dyubhele ; Linda Nelani ; Nelisa Sipamla ; ed.: Wendy Walton ; English-Isixhosa compiler: Mary Reynolds ; ed.: Sidney Zotwana ; translators: Fumanekile Dyubhele ; Nontembiso Jaxa ; Fikiswa Magqashela ; Linda Nelani ; Nelisa Sipamla ; [et al.]. – Cape Town : Oxford UP. Southern Africa, 2014. – 640 p.

819   Schryver, Gilles-Maurice de: Revolutionizing Bantu lexicography – a Zulu case study. – *Lexikos* 20, 2010, 161-201 | E. & Du. ab.

3.4.   TERMINOLOGY

820   Alberts, Mariëtta; Mollema, Nina: Developing legal terminology in African languages as aid to the court interpreter : a South African perspective. – *Lexikos* 23, 2013, 29-58 | Predominantly on Northern Sotho | E. & Afrikaans ab.

821   Koopman, Adrian: *Zulu plant names.* – Pietermaritzburg : University of Natal Press, 2015. – 324 p.

822   Mabule, D. R.: The taboos attached to the translation of biological terms from English into Northern Sotho. – *SAfrJAL* 29/1, 2009, 43-53.

823   Moyo, Nobuhle; Nkomo, Dion: Not mere lexicographic cosmetics : the compilation and structural features of *Isichazamazwi SezoMculo.* – *Lexikos* 19, Suppl., 2009, 51-70 | On a Ndebele musical terms dictionary.

824 Taljard, Elsabé: Cattle and their colours : a synchronic investigation of cattle colour terminology in Northern Sotho. – *SAfrJAL* 35/2, 2015, 199-205.

825 Taljard, Elsabé; Nchabeleng, Mahlodi Jean: Management and internal standardization of chemistry terminology : a Northern Sotho case study. – *Lexikos* 21, 2011, 194-216 | E. & Afrikaans ab.

3.5. PHRASEOLOGY, PAROEMIOLOGY

826 Mafela, Munzhedzi James: On the phraseology of Tshivenḓa idioms. – (86), 211-224 | E. & Pol. ab.

827 Possa, Rethabile Marriet: The form of contemporary Sesotho proverbs. – *SAfrJAL* 34/Suppl., 2014, 61-69.

4.1. SEMANTICS

828 Ngcobo, Mtholeni N: Zulu noun classes revisited : a spoken corpus-based approach. – *SAfrJAL* 30/1, 2010, 11-21.

829 Taljard, Elsabé: In search of larger units of meaning : a foray into Northern Sotho data. – *LM* 45/1, 2014, 91-109 | E. ab.

4.1.1. LEXICAL SEMANTICS

830 Bosch, Sonja E.; Pretorius, Laurette: A computational approach to Zulu verb morphology within the context of lexical semantics. – *Lexikos* 27, 2017, 152-182 | E. & Afrikaans ab.

831 Mathonsi, Nhlanhla: Semantic variation and the notion of polysemy in Zulu. – *SAfrJAL* 29/1, 2009, 87-95.

832 Nokele, Amanda B. B.: Identifying conceptual metaphors using the Metaphor Identification Procedure Vrije Universiteit (MIPVU). – *SAfrJAL* 34/1, 2014, 75-86 | On isiXhosa.

4.1.2. GRAMMATICAL SEMANTICS

833 [Groenewald, H. C.] Groenewald, Manie: Comments on 'A critique of "A re-evaluation of tense in isiZulu"' by Lionel Posthumus. – *Literator* 37/1, 2016, 2 p | Comm. on 835.

834 Groenewald, Hermanus C.: A re-evaluation of tenses in isiZulu. – *Literator* 35/1, 2014, 8 p | E. & Afrikaans ab.

835   Posthumus, Lionel C.: A critique of 'A re-evaluation of tense in isi-
       Zulu'. – *Literator* 37/1, 2016, 12 p | E. & Afrikaans ab | Comm. on 834.

836   Stavić, Stefan: The perfective and imperfective aspects in Xhosa. –
       SPILPLUS 52, 2017, 45-72 | E. ab.

4.2.   PRAGMATICS, DISCOURSE ANALYSIS AND TEXT GRAMMAR

837   Bagwasi, Mompoloki Mmangaka: Pragmatics of letter writing in
       Setswana. – *JoP* 40/3, 2008, 525-536 | Comparing English and Setswana
       letter writing in Botswana during the protectorate period (1885-1966).

838   Dlali, Mawande; Mogase, Phuti: The speech act of advice in Setswana
       educational contexts. – *SAfrJAL* 29/2, 2009, 145-157.

839   Gxowa-Dlayedwa, Ntombizodwa Cynthia: Identifying unmarked topi-
       cal thematic patterns : evidence from spoken and written isiXhosa
       texts. – *SAfrJAL* 33/2, 2013, 213-223.

840   Hendrikse, A. P.; Nomdebevana, N.; Allwood, Jens: An exploration of
       the nature, functions and subcategories of the discourse functional
       category, Interactive, in spoken Xhosa. – *SAfrJAL* 36/1, 2016, 93-101.

841   Kaschula, Russell H.; Mostert, André: The influence of cellular phone
       "speak" on isiXhosa rules of communication. – *SPILPLUS* 37, 2009,
       69-88.

842   Ndlovu, Manqoba Victor: Referential cohesion in isiZulu translated
       health texts. – *SALALS* 31/3, 2013, 349-357.

843   Ntombela, Sipho Albert: *Maskandi* : a critical discourse analysis of
       indigenous isiZulu songs. – *SALALS* 34/2, 2016, 109-120 | E. ab.

844   Sengani, Thomas M.: Controversies around the so-called allitera-
       tive concord in African languages : a critical language awareness on
       communicative competence with specific reference to Tshivenda. –
       SAfrJAL 33/2, 2013, 189-201.

845   Sengani, Thomas M.: Hidden dialogicality in *Mafhuwe* – a critical
       discourse analytical interpretation of struggles of power relations in
       Tshivenḓa women songs of protest. – *SAfrJAL* 31/2, 2011, 178-189.

7.   TRANSLATION

846   Mabule, D. R.: Issues involved in translating technical texts from
       English into Northern Sotho. – *SAfrJAL* 36/2, 2016, 217-224.

847   Madadzhe, Richard Ndwayamato; Mashamba, Mabula: Translation
       and cultural adaptation with specific reference to Tshivenda and
       English : a case of medical terms and expressions. – *SAfrJAL* 34/Suppl.,
       2014, 51-56.

848 Moropa, Koliswa: Utilizing 'hot words' in ParaConc to verify lexical simplification strategies in English-Xhosa parallel texts. – *SAfrJAL* 29/2, 2009, 227-241.

849 Wildsmith-Cromarty, Rosemary: Can academic/scientific discourse really be translated across English and African languages? – *SALALS* 26/1, 2008, 147-169 | On isiZulu, SeSotho & SeTswana.

8.1. ORTHOGRAPHY

850 Mabaso, X. E.: Some issues regarding the standardisation of the terminative vowel in Xitsonga. – *SAfrJAL* 37/2, 2017, 187-194 | E. ab.

851 Malambe, Gloria B.; Khumalo, Langa; Hoza, Mfusi; Ngubane, Sihawukele E.; Zulu, Nogwaja S.; Mazibuko, Guguethu; Vilakati, Sizakele; Phiri, Sellinah; Madonsela, Stanley; Nkomo, Dion; Gumede, Grace; Masilela, Piet; Madolo, Yolisa; Gxowa-Dlayedwa, Ntombizodwa Cynthia; Jokweni, Mbulelo W.: *A unified standard orthography for Nguni languages : South Africa, Swaziland, Zimbabwe, Tanzania, Malawi and Zambia.* – Cape Town : CASAS, 2013. – 30 p. – (Monograph series [CASAS] ; 255).

852 Musehane, Mbulaheni; Maṱhabi, Mashudu: Orthographic errors in written Tshivenḓa on funeral programmes of Vhembe District Municipality funeral undertakers. – *SAfrJAL* 36/2, 2016, 225-230.

853 Nkuna, Paul H.: Orthographic considerations regarding the class 4 noun prefix and some verb stems in Xitsonga. – *SAfrJAL* 33/1, 2013, 75-78.

8.2. PUNCTUATION

854 Chokoe, Sekgaila: Tlhalošontši ya mongwalo : go ngwala seo se sa tšweletšego molaetša ka tshwanelo. – *SAfrJAL* 37/2, 2017, 195-201 | Orthographic ambiguity : writing the unmeant | E. & Sotho ab.

9.2. PSYCHOLINGUISTICS

855 Bylund, Emanuel; Athanasopoulos, Panos: Language and thought in a multilingual context : the case of isiXhosa. – *Bilingualism* 17/2, 2014, 431-441.

856 Diemer, Maxine; Merwe, Kristin van der; Vos, Mark de: The development of phonological awareness literacy measures for isiXhosa. – *SALALS* 33/3, 2015, 325-341.

9.2.2.   LANGUAGE COMPREHENSION

857   Kgolo, Naledi; Eisenbeiß, Sonja: The role of morphological structure
       in the processing of complex forms : evidence from Setswana dever-
       bative nouns. – *LCN* 30/9, 2015, 1116-1133.

9.2.2.1.   PSYCHOLOGY OF READING

858   Fakude, Pheladi Florina: Reading comprehension trajectories in
       Sepedi : a case of rural grade 7 learners. – *SAfrJAL* 34/Suppl., 2014,
       23-27.
859   Hefer, Esté: Reading first and second language subtitles : Sesotho
       viewers reading in Sesotho and English. – *SALALS* 31/3, 2013, 359-373.
860   Hefer, Esté: Television subtitles and literacy : where do we go from
       here? – *JMMD* 34/7, 2013, 636-652.
861   Land, Sandra: Reading and the orthography of isiZulu. – *SAfrJAL* 35/2,
       2015, 163-175.
862   Rooy, Bertus van; Pretorius, Elizabeth J.: Is reading in an agglutinating
       language different from an analytic language? : an analysis of isiZulu
       and English reading based on eye movements. – *SALALS* 31/3, 2013,
       281-297.

9.3.   LANGUAGE ACQUISITION

863   Kline, Melissa; Demuth, Katherine: Factors facilitating implicit learn-
       ing : the case of the Sesotho passive. – *LAcq* 17/4, 2010, 220-234.

9.3.1.   FIRST LANGUAGE ACQUISITION, CHILD LANGUAGE

864   Dowling, Tessa; Gowlett, Derek F.: Problems in the acquisition of Noun
       Class 11 among Xhosa children. – *SALALS* 34/4, 2016, 289-309 | E. ab.
865   Gxilishe, Sandile: African languages, linguistics, child speech and
       speech pathology : the connection. – *PerLinguam* 24/2, 2008, 75-87 |
       E. ab.

9.3.1.1.   FIRST LANGUAGE ACQUISITION BY PRE-SCHOOL CHILDREN

866   Demuth, Katherine; Machobane, 'Malillo 'Matšepo; Moloi, Francina
       L.: Learning how to license null noun-class prefixes in Sesotho. –
       Language 85/4, 2009, 864-883.

867   Demuth, Katherine; Moloi, Francina L.; Machobane, 'Malillo 'Matšepo: 3-Year-olds' comprehension, production, and generalization of Sesotho passives. – *Cognition* 115/2, 2010, 238-251.

868   Demuth, Katherine; Weschler, Sara: The acquisition of Sesotho nominal agreement. – *Morphology* 22/1, 2012, 67-88.

869   Maphalala, Zinhle; Pascoe, Michelle; Smouse, Mantoa Rose: Phonological development of first language isiXhosa-speaking children aged 3;0–6;0 years : a descriptive cross-sectional study. – *CL&P* 28/3, 2014, 176-194.

870   Smouse, Mantoa Rose; Gxilishe, Sandile; Villiers, Jill G. de; Villiers, Peter A. de: Children's acquisition of subject markers in isiXhosa. – (90), 209-236.

871   Smouse, Mantoa Rose: Uninterpretable features in comprehension : subject-verb agreement in isiXhosa. – *SAfrJAL* 33/1, 2013, 65-74.

9.3.1.2.   FIRST LANGUAGE ACQUISITION BY SCHOOL CHILDREN

872   Kunene-Nicolas, Ramona N.; Guidetti, Michèle; Colletta, Jean-Marc: A cross-linguistic study of the development of gesture and speech in Zulu and French oral narratives. – *JChL* 44/1, 2017, 36-62 | E. ab.

873   Kunene-Nicolas, Ramona N.: Zulu oral narrative development from a speech and gesture perspective. – *PerLinguam* 31/3, 2015, 1-18 | E. ab.

874   Wilsenach, Carien: Phonological skills as predictor of reading success : an investigation of emergent bilingual Northern Sotho/English learners. – *PerLinguam* 29/2, 2013, 17-32 | E. ab.

9.3.2.   SECOND LANGUAGE ACQUISITION

875   Lombard, Shona; Conradie, Simone: L1 influence in the L2 acquisition of isiXhosa verb placement by English and Afrikaans adolescents. – *SPILPLUS* 38, 2009, 167-181 | E. ab.

9.3.2.2.   GUIDED SECOND LANGUAGE ACQUISITION

876   *Multilingual universities in South Africa : reflecting society in higher education* / Ed. by Liesel Hibbert ; Christa van der Walt. – Bristol : Multilingual Matters, 2014. – xii, 223 p. – (Bilingual education and bilingualism ; 97).

10.1.   SOCIOLINGUISTICS

877   Akindele, Femi Dele: Sesotho address forms. – *LO* 34/2, 2008, 3-15 |
      Electronic publ.

878   Bagwasi, Mompoloki Mmangaka: The effect of gender and age in
      Setswana greetings. – *SALALS* 30/1, 2012, 93-100.

879   Bagwasi, Mompoloki Mmangaka; Sunderland, Jane: Language, gender
      and age(ism) in Setswana. – (636), 53-78.

880   Beyer, Klaus: Urban language research in South Africa : achievements
      and challenges. – *SALALS* 32/2, 2014, 247-254.

881   Black, Steven P.: Narrating fragile stories about HIV/AIDS in South
      Africa. – *PrS* 4/3, 2013, 345-368.

882   Chebanne, Andy: Found and lost languages : survey of the past and
      current situation of Botswana ethic and linguistic communities. 48,
      2016, 160-175 | E. ab.

883   Coetzee-Van Rooy, Susan: The language repertoire of a Venda home
      language speaker : reflections on methodology. – *LM* 47/2, 2016, 269-
      296 | E. ab.

884   Dowling, Tessa: 'Hola, my new cherry!' : two case studies of isiXhosa
      advertising in print media. – *SAfrJAL* 33/2, 2013, 173-188.

885   Duran, Daniel; Bruni, Jagoda; Dogil, Grzegorz; Roux, Justus C.: The
      social life of Setswana ejectives. – *Interspeech*, 2017, 3787-3791 | E. ab.

886   Dyers, Charlyn; Davids, Gaironesa: Post-modern 'languagers' : the
      effects of texting by university students on three South African
      languages. – *SALALS* 33/1, 2015, 21-30 | On Afrikaans, isiXhosa and
      Setswana.

887   Engelbrecht, Charlotte; Nkosi, Zethu; Wentzel, Dorien; Govender,
      Selverani; McInerney, Patricia: Nursing students' use of language in
      communicating with isiZulu speaking clients in clinical settings in
      KwaZulu-Natal. – *SAfrJAL* 28/2, 2008, 145-155.

888   Hanong Thetela, Puleng: Sex discourses and the construction of gen-
      der identity in Sesotho : a case study of police interviews of rape/
      sexual assault victims. – (636), 205-215.

889   Hurst, Ellen: Overview of the tsotsitaals of South Africa; their differ-
      ent base languages and common core lexical items. – (104), 169-184.

890   Jadezweni, Mhlobo W.; Mfazwe-Mojapelo, Lungelwa Rose: Achieving
      public acceptability of taboo words translated into isiXhosa. – (632),
      201-223.

891   Kretzer, Michael M.: Variations of overt and covert language practices of educators in the North West Province : case study of the use of Setswana and Sesotho at primary and secondary schools. – *SAfrJAL* 36/1, 2016, 15-24.

892   Madadzhe, Richard Ndwayamato: Linguistic taboos in Tshivenḍa : communicating across epochs. – *SAfrJAL* 30/2, 2010, 108-191.

893   Madonsela, Stanley: A critical analysis of the use of code-switching in Nhlapho's novel *Imbali YemaNgcamane*. – *SAfrJAL* 34/2, 2014, 167-174.

894   Matlhaku, Keneilwe: Sociolinguistic factors in Setswana loanwords. – (632), 131-160.

895   Mkhize, Dumisile N.: Resources, mediators, and identities : home literacy practices of rural bilingual children. – *SALALS* 34/1, 2016, 43-55 | E. ab.

896   Msibi, Thabo: Homophobic language and linguistic resistance in KwaZulu-Natal, South Africa. – (636), 253-274.

897   Ndimande-Hlongwa, Nobuhle; Ndebele, Hloniphani: Digging deep into IsiZulu-English code-switching in a peri-urban context. – *LM* 45/2, 2014, 237-256 | E. ab.

898   Ndlovu, Sambulo: Thematic characterisation of Ndebele *izichothozo*. – *SAfrJAL* 35/1, 2015, 113-121.

899   Nhlekisana, Rosaleen O. B.: Language and gender in popular music in Botswana. – (636), 177-202.

900   Nkosi, Zinhle Primrose: IsiZulu as a vehicle towards teaching and conducting research in higher education : challenges and prospects. – *SAfrJAL* 37/2, 2017, 225-233 | E. ab.

901   Olivier, Jako: *Sesotho Online* : establishing an internet-based language knowledge community. – *SAfrJAL* 36/2, 2016, 141-152.

902   Posel, Dorrit; Zeller, Jochen: Home language and English language ability in South Africa : insights from new data. – *SALALS* 29/2, 2011, 115-126.

903   Rudwick, Stephanie Inge: Gendered linguistic choices among isiZulu-speaking women in contemporary South Africa. – (636), 233-251.

904   Rudwick, Stephanie Inge; Ntuli, Mduduzi: IsiNgqumo – introducing a gay Black South African linguistic variety. – *SALALS* 26/4, 2008, 445-456.

10.1.1.   LANGUAGE ATTITUDES AND SOCIAL IDENTITY

905   Banda, Felix; Peck, Amiena: Diversity and contested social identities in multilingual and multicultural contexts of the University of the Western Cape, South Africa. – *JMMD* 37/6, 2016, 576-588 | E. ab.

906   Beukes, Anne-Marie: 'The greasy pole of dehumanisation' : language and violence in South Africa. – *LM* 43/2, 2012, 128-145 | E. ab.

907   Black, Steven P.: Stigma and ideological constructions of the foreign : facing HIV/AIDS in South Africa. – *LiS* 42/5, 2013, 481-502 | E. ab.

908   Bristowe, Anthea; Oostendorp, Marcelyn; Anthonissen, Christine: Language and youth identity in a multilingual setting : a multimodal repertoire approach. – *SALALS* 32/2, 2014, 229-245.

909   Ditsele, Thabo: Attitudes held by Setswana L1-speaking university students toward their L1 : new variables. – *SAfrJAL* 36/1, 2016, 1-13.

910   Ditsele, Thabo: Testing the impact of known variables on the attitudes held by Setswana L1-speaking university students towards their L1. – *Literator* 38/1, 2017, 15 p | E. & Afrikaans ab.

911   Ditsele, Thabo: Why not use Sepitori to enrich the vocabularies of Setswana and Sepedi? – *SALALS* 32/2, 2014, 215-228.

912   Hilton, Nanna Haug: University students' context-dependent conscious attitudes towards the official South African languages. – *SALALS* 28/2, 2010, 123-132.

913   [Kamwendo, Gregory Hankoni] Kamwendo, Gregory; Hlongwa, Nobuhle; Mkhize, Nhlanhla: On medium of instruction and African scholarship : the case of Isizulu at the University of Kwazulu-Natal in South Africa. – *CILP* 15/1, 2014, 75-89.

914   Letsholo, Rose M.; Matlhaku, Keneilwe: Attitudes of University of Botswana Faculty of Humanities students towards minority languages. – *SALALS* 35/3, 2017, 245-257 | E. ab.

915   Lombard, Ellen: Students' attitudes and preferences toward language of learning and teaching at the University of South Africa. – *LM* 48/3, 2017, 25-48 | E. ab.

916   Mbatha, T. A.: Ideologies shaping language choices : views of African students on Isizulu modules in higher education at the University of Kwazulu-Natal. – *NJAS* 25/2, 2016, 146-166 | E. ab.

917   Mojela, V. M.: Standardization or stigmatization? : challenges confronting lexicography and terminography in Sesotho sa Leboa. – *Lexikos* 18, 2008, 119-130 | E. & Afrikaans ab.

918   Moodley, Dianna Lynette: Bilingualism gridlocked at the University of KwaZulu-Natal. – *NJAS* 18/1, 2009, 22-27 | Electronic publ.

919   Msibi, Thabo; Rudwick, Stephanie Inge: Intersections of two isiZulu genderlects and the construction of *skesana* identities. – *SPILPLUS* 46, 2015, 51-66 | E. ab.

920   [Neethling, Siebert J.] Neethling, Bertie: Bynames as an expression of identity : a student profile at the University of the Western Cape. – (4), 23-38 | On Xhosa, Afrikaans and English names.

921   [Neethling, Siebert J.] Neethling, Bertie: Naming in the Muslim and Xhosa communities : a comparative analysis. – *SAfrJAL* 32/2, 2012, 161-166.

922   Nkosi, Zinhle Primrose: Postgraduate students' experiences and attitudes towards isiZulu as a medium of instruction at the University of KwaZulu-Natal. – *CILP* 15/3, 2014, 245-264.

923   Rudwick, Stephanie Inge; Parmegiani, Andrea: Divided loyalties : Zulu vis-à-vis English at the University of KwaZulu-Natal. – *LM* 44/3, 2013, 89-107 | E. ab.

924   Rudwick, Stephanie Inge: Shifting norms of linguistic and cultural respect : hybrid sociolinguistic Zulu identities. – *NJAS* 17/2, 2008, 152-174 | Electronic publ.

925   Rudwick, Stephanie Inge: Zulu Varietäten als Ausdruck unterschiedlicher Kulturansprüche und Geschlechterverhältnisse im heutigen Südafrika. – *ArOr* 79/1, 2011, 27-45 | E. ab.

926   Siziba, Gugulethu: Language and identity negotiations : an analysis of the experiences of Zimbabwean migrants in Johannesburg, South Africa. – *JACS* 26/2, 2014, 173-188 | E. & Zulu ab.

927   Stell, Gerald: Ethnicity and codeswitching : ethnic differences in grammatical and pragmatic patterns of codeswitching in the Free State. – *Pragmatics* 22/3, 2012, 477-499.

928   Thamaga-Chitja, J. M.; [Mbatha, T. A.] Mbatha, T.: Enablers and barriers to multilingualism in South African university classrooms. – *SALALS* 30/3, 2012, 339-346 | On Zulu and English.

929   Wildsmith-Cromarty, Rosemary; Conduah, Aloysius N.: Issues of identity and African unity surrounding the introduction of an exogenous African language, Swahili, at tertiary level in South Africa. – *IJBEB* 17/6, 2014, 638-653 | E. ab.

10.1.2.   LANGUAGE POLICY AND LANGUAGE PLANNING

930   Alberts, Mariëtta: National language and terminology policies – a South African perspective. – *Lexikos* 20, 2010, 599-620 | E. & Afrikaans ab.

931   Amtaika, Alexius: The power and authority of the dominant to name : a case study of selected Nyanja and isiZulu linguistic expressions regarding 'national assets'. – *JACS* 26/1, 2014, 99-115.

932   Beukes, Anne-Marie: Challenges for South Africa's medium-sized indigenous languages in higher education and research environments. – (117), 132-151.

933   Deumert, Ana: *Imbodela zamakhumsha* : reflections on standardization and destandardization. – *Multilingua* 29/3-4, 2010, 243-264 | Evidence from isiXhosa.

934   Hadebe, Vusumuzi: Communication policy and communication practice within the eThekwini Municipality. – *SAfrJAL* 29/2, 2009, 158-168.

935   Heugh, Kathleen: Harmonisation and South African languages : twentieth century debates of homogeneity and heterogeneity. – *LPol* 15/3, 2016, 235-255 | E. ab.

936   Hornberger, Nancy H.: On not taking language inequality for granted : Hymesian traces in ethnographic monitoring of South Africa's multilingual language policy. – *Multilingua* 33/5-6, 2014, 623-645.

937   Kadenge, Maxwell: "Where art thou Sesotho?" : exploring the linguistic landscape of Wits University. – *PerLinguam* 31/1, 2015, 30-45 | E. ab.

938   Kamwendo, Gregory Hankoni; Dlamini, Nosisi Percis: Language planning at a cross-border university in Swaziland : the case of teaching and learning, research and institutional administration. – *CILP* 17/3-4, 2016, 298-310 | E. ab.

939   Khumalo, Langa: Intellectualization through terminology development. – *Lexikos* 27, 2017, 252-264 | E. & Afrikaans ab.

940   Mabuto, Morgen Peter; Ndlovu, Sambulo: Teaching under-resourced languages : an evaluation of Great Zimbabwe University's initiatives in the teaching of Tshivenda and Xichangana. – *SAfrJAL* 34/1, 2014, 1-8.

941   Masoke-Kadenge, Emure; Kadenge, Maxwell: 'Declaration without implementation' : an investigation into the progress made and challenges faced in implementing the Wits language policy. – *LM* 44/3, 2013, 33-50 | E. ab.

942   Mesthrie, Rajend: Necessary versus sufficient conditions for using new languages in South African higher education : a linguistic appraisal. – *JMMD* 29/4, 2008, 325-340 | On the developing of Xhosa as a scientific language.

943   Mgqwashu, Emmanuel Mfanafuthi: On developing academic literacy in the mother tongue for epistemological access : the role of isiZulu as the LoLT in a South African University. – *CILP* 15/1, 2014, 90-103.

944   Mokibelo, Eureka B.: Communication strategies in primary schools in Botswana : interventions using cooks, teacher aides and learners. – *CILP* 17/2, 2016, 179-190 | E. ab.

945 Mutasa, Davie E.: Language policy implementation in South African universities vis-a-vis the speakers of indigenous African languages' perception. – *PerLinguam* 31/1, 2015, 46-59 | E. ab.

946 Mutasa, Davie E.: Multilingual education in South African universities : a possibility or delusion? – *SAfrJAL* 34/1, 2014, 9-20.

947 Ndlovu, Eventhough: Mother tongue education in the official minority languages in Zimbabwe. – *SAfrJAL* 31/2, 2011, 229-242 | On Venda, Tonga, Nambya, Kalanga, Sotho and Shangani.

948 Ndlovu, Eventhough: Mother-tongue education in Venda : an ethnolinguistic vitality critique. – *LM* 46/3, 2015, 364-388 | E. ab.

949 [Neethling, Siebert J] Neethling, Bertie: Xhosa as medium of instruction in Higher Education : pie in the sky? – *PerLinguam* 26/1, 2010, 61-73 | E. ab.

950 Ngcobo, Sandiso: The struggle to maintain identity in higher education among Zulu-speaking students. – *IJBEB* 17/6, 2014, 695-713 | E. ab.

951 Phaahla, Pinkie: Economics of languages : the interplay between language planning and policy, and language practice in South Africa. – *SAfrJAL* 35/2, 2015, 181-188.

952 Pillay, Venitha; Yu, Ke: Multilingualism at South African universities : a quiet storm. – *SALALS* 33/4, 2015, 439-452.

953 Plessis, Theodorus du: Language planning from below : the case of the Xhariep District of the Free State Province. – *CILP* 11/2, 2010, 130-151.

954 Plessis, Theodorus du: The role of language policy in linguistic landscape changes in a rural area of the Free State Province of South Africa. – *LM* 43/2, 2012, 263-282 | E. ab.

955 Plessis, Theodorus du: The South African Language Rights Monitor and information on language policy and planning in South Africa. – *LM* 45/3, 2014, 378-400 | E. ab.

956 Pretorius, Elizabeth J.: Failure to launch : matching language policy with literacy accomplishment in South African schools. – *IJSL* 234, 2015, 47-76.

957 Ralarala, Monwabisi Knowledge: A compromise of rights, rights of language and rights to a language in Eugene Terre'Blanche's (ET) trial within a trial : evidence lost in translation. – *SPIL* 41, 2012, 55-70 | E. ab.

958 Ranamane, Tlhabane D.: The contribution of the missionaries to the development of Setswana as a written language. – *SAfrJAL* 32/1, 2012, 27-33.

959 Rudwick, Stephanie Inge: Compulsory African language learning at a South African university. – *LPLP* 41/2, 2017, 115-135 | E., Zulu & Esperanto ab.

960   Turner, Noleen S.; Wildsmith-Cromarty, Rosemary: Challenges to the implementation of bilingual/multilingual language policies at tertiary institutions in South Africa (1995–2012). – *LM* 45/3, 2014, 295-312 | E. ab.

961   [Webb, Victor] Webb, Vic: Educators' attitudes towards the role of isiZulu in education : additive rather than exclusive. – *SALALS* 31/2, 2013, 185-205.

10.1.4.   LANGUAGE LOSS AND MAINTENANCE

962   Deumert, Ana: Xhosa in town (revisited) : space, place and language. – *IJSL* 222, 2013, 51-75.

963   Möller, Jana; Le Roux, Beth: Implementing constitutional language provisions through the Indigenous Language Publishing Programme. – *SAfrJAL* 37/2, 2017, 203-209 | E. ab.

964   Yu, Ke; Dumisa, Siphesihle: Community support : the missing link in indigenous language promotion in South Africa? – *PerLinguam* 31/1, 2015, 60-73 | E. ab.

10.2.   MULTILINGUALISM, LANGUAGE CONTACT

965   Bylund, Emanuel: *Unomathotholo* or *i-radio*? : factors predicting the use of English loanwords among L1 isiXhosa–L2 English bilinguals. – *JMMD* 35/2, 2014, 105-120.

10.2.1.   MULTILINGUALISM

966   Anthonissen, Christine: Managing linguistic diversity in a South African HIV/AIDS day clinic. – (132), 107-139 | E. ab.

967   Dowling, Tessa: Translated for the dogs : language use in Cape Town signage. – *LM* 43/2, 2012, 240-262 | E. ab.

968   Dowling, Tessa: *'Welcome to proper mall'* : the language on signs in Diepsloot, Johannesburg. – *SAfrJAL* 34/1, 2014, 87-95.

969   Johanson Botha, Liz: *Language learning, power, race and identity : white men, black language.* – Bristol : Multilingual Matters, 2015. – xxv, 262 p. – (Encounters ; 4).

970   Kaschula, Russell H.; Maseko, Pamela; Dalvit, Lorenzo; Mapi, Thandeka; Nelani, Linda; Nosilela, Bulelwa; Sam, Msindisi: An intercultural approach to implementing multilingualism at Rhodes University, South Africa. – *SPILPLUS* 39, 2009, 45-61.

971 Ndimande-Hlongwa, Nobuhle; Ndebele, Hloniphani: Embracing African languages as indispensable resources through the promotion of multilingualism. – *PerLinguam* 33/1, 2017, 67-82 | E. ab.

972 Phaahla, Pinkie: Multilingualism in a global village : what is the future of a local language (e.g. Northern Sotho) in an increasingly globalized world? – *SAfrJAL* 30/1, 2010, 52-65.

973 Posel, Dorrit; Zeller, Jochen: Language shift or increased bilingualism in South Africa : evidence from census data. – *JMMD* 37/4, 2016, 357-370 | E. ab.

974 Sobane, Konosoang: Multilingual practices and language scaling in behavioural change communication on HIV/AIDS in Lesotho : the case of Phela health and development communications. – *SPILPLUS* 41, 2012, 107-115 | E. ab.

10.2.3. LANGUAGE CONTACT

975 Andrason, Alexander: The "exotic" nature of ideophones : from Khoekhoe to Xhosa. – *SPIL* 48, 2017, 139-150 | E. ab.

976 Ditsele, Thabo; Mann, Charles C.: Language contact in African urban settings : the case of Sepitori in Tshwane. – *SAfrJAL* 34/2, 2014, 159-165 | Sepitori is a mixed lg. based on Sepedi and Setswana.

977 Mahlangu, K. S.: Language contact and linguistic change : the case of Afrikaans and English influence on isiNdebele. – *SAfrJAL* 36/1, 2016, 25-31.

978 Maimane, Ketlalemang; Mathonsi, Nhlanhla: Phonological adaptations of foreign names into Sesotho : anthroponyms and toponyms. – *NAfr* 31/2, 2017, 183-190 | E. ab.

979 Mesthrie, Rajend: Pidginization versus second language acquisition : insights from basilang and mesolang varieties of Zulu as a second language. – (50), 323-342 | E. ab.

980 Ngcobo, Mtholeni N: Loan words classification in isiZulu : the need for a sociolinguistic approach. – *LM* 44/1, 2013, 21-38 | E. ab.

981 Pakendorf, Brigitte; Gunnink, Hilde; Sands, Bonny; Bostoen, Koen: Prehistoric Bantu-Khoisan language contact : a cross-disciplinary approach. – *LgDC* 7/1, 2017, 1-46 | E. ab.

982 Simango, Silvester Ron: "*Amaphi ama*-subjects *eniwa*-enjoy-*ayo esikolweni*?" : code-switching and language practices among bilingual learners in the Eastern Cape. – *IJSL* 234, 2015, 77-91.

983   Simango, Silvester Ron: When English meets isiXhosa in the clause :
       an exploration into the grammar of code-switching. – *SALALS* 29/2,
       2011, 127-134.

984   Zsiga, Elizabeth C.; Boyer, One Tlale: Sebirwa in contact with
       Setswana : a natural experiment in learning an unnatural alterna-
       tion. – (633), 343-366 | E. ab.

10.4. DIALECTOLOGY

985   Mulaudzi, Phalandwa Abraham: Cross-border language varieties : the
       case of Tshilembethu and Lembethu/ Chilembethu and their rela-
       tionship with Tshivenḓa. – *SALALS* 29/4, 2011, 435-446.

11. COMPARATIVE LINGUISTICS

986   Andrason, Alexander; Visser, Marianna W.: Cognate objects of
       weather verbs in African languages of South Africa : from synchronic
       variation to a grammaticalization path. – *SPIL* 48, 2017, 151-160 | E. ab.

987   Ma, Xiujie; Simango, Silvester Ron: Encoding present situations in
       Mandarin Chinese and isiXhosa : a comparative study. – *SPIL* 43, 2014,
       119-135 | E. ab.

11.1. HISTORICAL LINGUISTICS AND LANGUAGE CHANGE

988   Batibo, Herman M.: The origin and evolution of Setswana culture : a
       linguistic account. 48, 2016, 134-149 | E. ab.

11.2. LINGUISTIC TYPOLOGY, UNIVERSALS OF LANGUAGE

989   *The conjoint/disjoint alternation in Bantu* / Ed. by Jenneke van der Wal
       and Larry M. Hyman. – Berlin : De Gruyter Mouton, 2017. – x, 458 p. –
       (Trends in linguistics. Studies and monographs ; 301).

12. MATHEMATICAL AND COMPUTATIONAL LINGUISTICS

990   Faaß, Gertrud; Bosch, Sonja E.; Taljard, Elsabé: Towards a part-of-
       speech ontology : encoding morphemic units of two South African
       Bantu languages. – *NJAS* 21/3, 2012, 118-140 | Electronic publ.

991   Taljard, Elsabé; Faaß, Gertrud; Bosch, Sonja E.: Implementation of a part-of-speech ontology : morphemic units of Bantu languages. – *NJAS* 24/2, 2015, 146-168 | E. ab.

12.2.1.   CORPUS LINGUISTICS

992   Bosch, Sonja E.; Pretorius, Laurette: Towards Zulu corpus clean-up, lexicon development and corpus annotation by means of computational morphological analysis. – *SAfrJAL* 31/1, 2011, 138-158.

993   Ndhlovu, Ketiwe: Using ParaConc to extract bilingual terminology from parallel corpora : a case of English and Ndebele. – *Literator* 37/2, 2016, 12 p | E. & Afrikaans ab.

994   Niekerk, Daniel van; Heerden, Charl van; Davel, Marelie; Kleynhans, Neil; Kjartansson, Oddur; Jansche, Martin; Ha, Linne: Rapid development of TTS corpora for four South African languages. – *Interspeech*, 2017, 2178-2182 | Afrikaans, isiXhosa, Sesotho and Setswana | E. ab.

995   Taljard, Elsabé; Faaß, Gertrud; Heid, Ulrich; Prinsloo, D. J.: On the development of a tagset for Northern Sotho with special reference to the issue of standardisation. – *Literator* 29/1, 2008, 111-137 | E. & Afrikaans ab.

12.3.   COMPUTATIONAL LINGUISTICS

996   Anderson, Winston N.; Kotzé, Albert E.: Verbal extension sequencing : an examination from a computational perspective. – *Literator* 29/1, 2008, 43-63 | E. & Afrikaans ab.

997   Bosch, Sonja E.; Fellbaum, Christiane; Pala, Karel: Derivational relations in English, Czech and Zulu wordnets. – *Literator* 29/1, 2008, 139-162 | E. & Afrikaans ab.

998   Bosch, Sonja E.; Griesel, Marissa: Strategies for building wordnets for under-resourced languages : the case of African languages. – *Literator* 38/1, 2017, 12 p. | E. & Afrikaans ab.

999   Bosch, Sonja E.; Pretorius, Laurette; Fleisch, Axel: Experimental bootstrapping of morphological analysers for Nguni languages. – *NJAS* 17/2, 2008, 66-88 | Electronic publ.

1000   Faaß, Gertrud; Prinsloo, D. J.: A computational implementation of the Northern Sotho infinitive. – *SAfrJAL* 31/2, 2011, 281-301.

1001   Glarner, Thomas; Boenninghoff, Benedikt; Walter, Oliver; Haeb-
        Umbach, Reinhold: Leveraging text data for word segmentation
        for underresourced languages. – *Interspeech*, 2017, 2143-2147 |
        Experiments with Xitsonga and English | E. ab.

1002   Heid, Ulrich; Prinsloo, D. J.; Faaß, Gertrud; Taljard, Elsabé: Designing a
        noun guesser for part of speech tagging in Northern Sotho. – *SAfrJAL*
        29/1, 2009, 1-19.

1003   Pretorius, Laurette; Bosch, Sonja E.: Containing overgeneration in
        Zulu computational morphology. – *SALALS* 26/2, 2008, 209-216.

1004   Pretorius, Laurette; Viljoen, Biffie; Berg, Ansu; Pretorius, Rigardt:
        Tswana finite state tokenisation. – *LRE* 49/4, 2015, 831-856 | E. ab.

1005   Pretorius, Laurette; Viljoen, Biffie; Pretorius, Rigardt; Berg, Ansu:
        Towards a computational morphological analysis of Setswana com-
        pounds. – *Literator* 29/1, 2008, 1-20 | E. & Afrikaans ab.

1006   Prinsloo, D. J.; Faaß, Gertrud; Taljard, Elsabé; Heid, Ulrich: Designing
        a verb guesser for part of speech tagging in Northern Sotho. – *SALALS*
        26/2, 2008, 185-196.

1007   Schlünz, Georg I.; Dlamini, Nkcsikhona; Krüger, Rynhardt P.: Part-of-
        speech tagging and chunking in text-to-speech synthesis for South
        African languages. – *Interspeech*, 2016, 3554-3558 | E. ab.

1008   Westhuizen, Ewald van der; Niesler, Thomas: Synthesising isiZulu-
        English code-switch bigrams using word embeddings. – *Interspeech*,
        2017, 72-76 | E. ab.

13.1. ANTHROPONYMY

1009   Bagwasi, Mompoloki Mmangaka: The influence of multilingualism,
        Christianity and education in the formation of Bakalanga identity. –
        IJEL 2/2, 2012, 122-131.

1010   Koopman, Adrian: Uniqueness in the Zulu anthroponymic system. –
        Onoma 44, 2009 [2011], 69-91 | E., G. & Fr. ab.

1011   Mandende, Itani Peter: *A study of Tshivenda personal names.* –
        Pretoria : Univ. of South Africa, 2009. – x, 222 p. | Diss. at Univ. of South
        Africa, June 2009.

1012   Matlosa, Lits'episo: Sesotho orthography called into question : the
        case of some Sesotho personal names. – *NAfr* 31/1, 2017, 51-58 | E. ab.

1013   [Neethling, Siebert J.] Neethling, Bertie: Family names among the
        Xhosa of South Africa. – *Onoma* 44, 2009 [2011], 107-128 | E., G. &
        Fr. ab.

1014   [Neethling, Siebert J.] Neethling, Bertie: Xhosa first names : a dual identity in harmony or in conflict? – *Names* 56/1, 2008, 32-38.

1015   [Neethling, Siebert J.] Neethling, Bertie: Xhosa onomastics as part of indigenous knowledge systems (IKS). – *Names* 62/4, 2014, 218-228.

1016   Ngubane, Sihawukele E.: The socio-cultural and linguistic implications of Zulu names. – *SAfrJAL* 33/2, 2013, 165-172.

1017   Ngubane, Sihawukele E.; Thabethe, Nompumelelo: Shifts and continuities in Zulu personal naming practices. – *Literator* 34/1, 2013, 7 p. | E. & Afrikaans ab.

1018   Zulu, Nogwaja S.; Makoae, Aloysia Sebueng: Analysis of the metaphorical expression *bitsolebe ke seromo* in early Sesotho novels. – *NAfr* 31/1, 2017, 29-37 | E. ab.

13.2.   TOPONYMY

1019   Koopman, Adrian: The names and the naming of Durban. – *Onoma* 42, 2007 (2010), 73-88 | E., Fr. & G. ab.

1020   Koopman, Adrian: The post-colonial identity of Durban. – *OSLa* 4/2, 2012, 133-159 | Electronic publ.

1021   [Meiring, Babs] Meiring, Barbara A.: Aspects of violence reflected in South African geographical names. – *Werkwinkel* 5/1, 2010, 95-112 | E. ab.

1022   Raper, Peter E.: The component Kwa- in Zulu placenames derived from Khoisan. – *Names* 57/3, 2009, 127-140.

1023   Raper, Peter E.: Descriptive Zulu placenames of San origin. – *Names* 57/1, 2009, 3-16.

13.3.   NAME STUDIES OTHER THAN ANTHROPONYMY AND TOPONYMY

1024   Babane, Morris T.; Chauke, Mkhacani T.: The sociocultural aspects of Xitsonga dog names. – *NAfr* 31/1, 2017, 59-67 | E. ab.

1025   Koopman, Adrian: The toponymic status of Zulu school and shop names. – *Onoma* 44, 2009 [2011], 55-67 | E., Fr. & G. ab.

1026   Koopman, Adrian: Zulu cattle names. – *BNF* 50/3-4, 2015, 319-333.

3.   Khoisan

1027   Besten, Hans den: The Dutch pidgins of the Old Cape colony. – (509), 95-121 | Translation of LB 1992, 22932.

1028   *Beyond 'Khoisan' : historical relations in the Kalahari Basin* / Ed. by
        Tom Güldemann ;Anne-Maria Fehn. – Amsterdam : Benjamins,
        2014. – xii, 331 p. – (Current issues in linguistic theory ; 330).

1029   Blench, Roger M.: Was there an interchange between Cushitic pasto-
        ralists and Khoisan speakers in the prehistory of Southern Africa and
        how this can be detected? – *SUGIA* 20, 2009, 31-49.

1030   Chebanne, Andy; Dlali, Mawande: Tsua lexical borrowing from
        Setswana. – *SAfrJAL* 37/1, 2017, 99-107 | E. ab.

1031   Chebanne, Andy: The !Xóõ-English-Setswana Trilingual Dictionary in
        preparation : an experience. – (51), 71-88.

1032   Haacke, Wilfried H. G.; Eiseb, Eliphas; Gericke, Christine:
        *Khoekhoegowab-Afrikaans : glossarium = Afrikaans-Khoekhoegowab :
        mîdi saogub.* – Windhoek, Namibia : Macmillan Education Namibia,
        2010. – vii, 407 p.

1033   Haacke, Wilfried H. G.: Lexical borrowing by Khoekhoegowab from
        Cape Dutch and Afrikaans. – *SPILPLUS* 47, 2015, 59-74 | E. ab.

1034   Haacke, Wilfried H. G.: *Nama* als Sprachbennenung in der
        Kolonallinguistik Deutsch-Südwestafrikas : zwischen Endonym und
        Exonym. – (52), 139-160.

1035   Haacke, Wilfried H. G.: Verb serialisation in northern dialects of
        Khoekhoegowab : convergence or divergence? – (1028), 125-152.

1036   Heine, Bernd; König, Christa: Observations on observations : on typo-
        logical features of hunter-gatherer languages. – (16), 127-143 | On Akie,
        !Xun, ǁAni, Kalenjin and Nama | E. ab.

1037   Ketsi, Kavila Lititinga; Cassanga, Antonio Luciano; Cativa, Manuel;
        Domingas, Helena; Tchilunda, Fernando: *Ortografia padrão unificada
        da língua !Xun : orthografia padrão unificada das língua Khoi e San
        (África do Sul, Angola, Botswana e Namibia)* / António Ndalo (falante
        mais velho). – Cape Town : CASAS, 2014. – iii, 24 p. – (Monograph
        series [CASAS] ; 259) | [Unified standard spelling of the !Xun lan-
        guage : unified standard spelling of the Khoi and San languages
        (South Africa, Angola, Botswana and Namibia)].

1038   McGranaghan, Mark: 'My name did float along the road' : naming
        practices and ǀXam Bushman identities in the 19th-century Karoo
        (South Africa). – *AfrS* 74/3, 2015, 270-289.

1039   Raper, Peter E.: Tshwane, a San name for Pretoria, South Africa. –
        Names 56/4, 2008, 221-230.

1040   Seidel, A.: *Nama (Sprache der Nama-Hottentotten) : kurzgefaßte Grammatik, analysierte Lesestücke nebst einem nama-deutschen und deutsch-nama Wörterbuch.* – München : LINCOM Europa, 2011. – 68 p. – (LINCOM gramatica ; 103) | Originally publ. in Vienna, 1892.

1041   *Southern African Khoisan kinship systems* / Alan Barnard ; Gertrud Boden (eds.). – Köln : Köppe, 2014. – 301 p. – (Quellen zur Khoian-Forschung = Researcin Khoisan studies ; 30) | References, p. 281-301.

1042   Vossen, Rainer: Patterns of linguistic convergence in the Khoe-speaking area of Southern Africa. – (13), 189-200.

Pidgins and Creoles

1043 *Deconstructing creole* / Ed. by Umberto Ansaldo ; Stephen Matthews ; Lisa Lim. – Amsterdam : Benjamins, 2007. – xi, 290 p. – (Typological studies in language ; 73).

1044 *Pidgins and creoles beyond Africa-Europe encounters* / Ed. by Isabelle Buchstaller ; Anders Holmberg ; Mohammad Almoaily. – Amsterdam : Benjamins, 2014. – v, 178 p. – (Creole language library ; 47).

1045 Roberge, Paul T.: Foundations of a "sane creology". – *Diachronica* 29/3, 2012, 359-376 | Rev. art. of 37.

1. Romance lexifier pidgins and creoles

1046 Besten, Hans den: Creole Portuguese in South Africa : Malayo- or Indo-Portuguese? – (509), 289-312 | Transl. of 1047.

1047 Besten, Hans den: Kreolportugiesisch in Südafrika : Malaio- oder Indoportugiesisch? – (1), 317-352.

2. English lexifier pidgins and creoles

1048 Mesthrie, Rajend: English tsotsitaals? : an analysis of two written texts in Surfspeak and South African Indian English slang. – *SALALS* 32/2, 2014, 173-183.

3. Pidgins and creoles with lexifiers other than Romance and English

1049 Besten, Hans den: On the "verbal suffix" -um of Cape Dutch Pidgin : morphosyntax, pronunciation and origin. – (509), 123-132 | First publ. in 42.

1050 Besten, Hans den: What we seem to know about the lexicon of Early Cape Dutch Pidgin (and always were afraid to question). – (51), 33-48.

1051   Mesthrie, Rajend: How non-Indo-European is Fanakalo pidgin? :
        selected understudied structures in a Bantu-lexified pidgin with
        Germanic substrates. – (1044), 85-100.

1052   Stell, Gerald: Social mobility as a factor in restructuring : Black Cape
        Dutch in perspective. – *JPCL* 32/1, 2017, 104-137 | E. ab.

Sign languages

2. Individual sign languages (except ASL)

1053   Baker, Anne Edith: Poetry in South African Sign Language : what is different? – *SPIL* 48, 2017, 87-92 | E. ab.

1054   Barros, Courtney de; Siebörger, Ian: Sentential negation in South African Sign Language : a case study. – *Literator* 37/2, 2016, 13 p | E. & Afrikaans ab.

1055   Huddlestone, Kate: A preliminary look at negative constructions in South African Sign Language : question-answer clauses. – *SPIL* 48, 2017, 93-104 | E. ab.

1056   Köhlo, Mikhaela D. K.; Siebörger, Ian; Bennett, William G.: A perfect end : a study of syllable codas in South African Sign Language. – *SPILPLUS* 52, 2017, 127-156 | E. ab.

1057   Morgan, Ruth; Glaser, Meryl; Magongwa, Lucas: Constructing and rolling out the new South African Sign Language (SASL) curriculum : reflexive critique. – *PerLinguam* 32/2, 2016, 15-29 | E. ab.

1058   Reagan, Timothy G.: South African Sign Language and language-in-education policy in South Africa. – *SPIL* 38, 2008, 165-190.

1059   Stander, Marga; McIlroy, Guy: Language and culture in the Deaf community : a case study in a South African special school. – *PerLinguam* 33/1, 2017, 83-99 | E. ab.

INDEX OF NAMES

This index contains the names of all authors, editors, etc., represented in the main part of this volume. Also included are names of persons who are the main subject of a publication. Names are listed alphabetically by surname.

INDEX OF NAMES

INDEX OF NAMES

INDEX OF NAMES

INDEX OF NAMES

INDEX OF NAMES

INDEX OF LANGUAGES

This index contains languages, language families, dialects, regiolects and language (sub)systems. When a language is not mentioned in the table of contents, information on its affiliation is added in brackets.

INDEX OF LANGUAGES

INDEX OF SUBJECTS

Printed in the United States
By Bookmasters